Effective Resumes for Executives and Specialized Personnel

SECOND EDITION

J.L. Angel

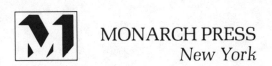

MONARCH PRESS
New York

Published by
MONARCH PRESS
a Simon & Schuster Division of Gulf & Western Corporation
Simon & Schuster Building
1230 Avenue of the Americas
New York, N.Y. 10020

MONARCH PRESS and colophon are trademarks of Simon & Schuster,
registered in the U.S. Patent and Trademark Office.

Printed in the United States of America

10   9   8   7   6   5

Library of Congress Cataloging in Publication Data

Angel, Juvenal Londoño, 1907- 1980

  Effective resumes for executives and specialized personnel.

  First ed. published in 1967 under title: Specialized resumes for executives
and professionals.
  1. Resumes (Employment) 2. Applications for positions. 3. Executives. I.
Title.
HF5383.A57 1980   650©.14   79-3255
ISBN 0-671-18782-1

CONTENTS

Introduction

IN PREPARING THIS SECOND EDITION of *Effective Resumes for Executives and Specialized Personnel,* special attention is given to the most up-to-date methods for preparing resumes. *Effective Resumes for Executives and Specialized Personnel* details how to compose a resume that will result in that all-important interview. It takes you from the initial step, a consideration of the directions that are open to you, to the final step, putting the final production touches on your resume.

The number of executives in administrative, managerial, and related positions in the United States is increasing rapidly. How does one choose from this growing forest of jobs? The first step is to stand back and look at jobs in their broad groupings—jobs that have similar standards for entrance requirements and that offer a similar way of life or work at desirable earnings.

The real challenge lies in locating a position that utilizes your capabilities and provides you with the greatest possible opportunity for advancement. To accomplish this, it is necessary to find the right position in the right company and then secure an interview with an officer in that company. Submission of a resume is a major step in this process.

An effective and well-prepared resume is the most important step in your campaign to find a better job. The resume is the key that will open the door to the most demanding employer or executive recruiter.

This step-by-step manual provides a comprehensive guide to obtaining the position best suited to your individual talents, temperament, and training. The self-marketing methods described in these pages have proven highly successful in the past. The advice offered for developing, organizing, and implementing a job campaign is combined with warnings against pitfalls that can hinder your search.

Exhaustive research has been conducted to update this edition, and new material has been added that we believe will be effective in obtaining a better position. The style, content, and format of these resumes are designed to impress leading corporations in the United States and highly selective international companies. All names used are fictitious.

Thanks are due to June L. Aulick for her constructive criticism of the manuscript, to Mark B. Heally for showing me the need for such a book and for suggestions during its preparation, and to Gloria C. Sainz, who helped in the preparation of the copy.

J.L. ANGEL

1

Conducting the Job Search

WHEN YOU LOOK FOR A JOB, you are conducting a campaign to sell yourself. You need to think of yourself as merchandise that must be carefully packaged and marketed. Your aim is to convince a prospective employer that you—and you alone—with your unique combination of skills, talents, and experience—are a good investment. And, as in any kind of sales, the first rule is to know your product. To sell yourself, you must know yourself.

Self-Evaluation—The First Step to Job Hunting

Begin by taking an inventory of your assets. It can be a mental list, or you can write the facts about yourself down on paper. The list will certainly be more concrete if you commit it to writing.

List details of your experience, projects on which you have worked, goals, ideas for your field, details of your education, and personality traits. Little of this information will actually appear on your resume in its final form, but you may nonetheless need to come up with some obscure fact about yourself when you are being interviewed. If you have carefully reviewed everything about you that might be relevant in looking for a new position, then it will be fresh in your mind during an interview.

Interviewing approaches vary as widely as employers do. Not every person who interviews you will want to know the same things about you. One interviewer may place more emphasis on education than on your job experience. Another may stress your previous work record. Some may be keenly interested in your extracurricular activities; others will seek information regarding your family background and your personality.

The key to a successful interview is to develop the ability to supply any piece of information or fact about yourself that an interviewer wants to hear. If you have drawn up the suggested lists about yourself, this information should be fresh in your mind and ready for instant use. Since you never know beforehand what you will be asked, you must be thoroughly armed with pertinent and accurate material about yourself. The reply to one question may make the difference between success or failure in your job search.

The information should be organized with a job goal in mind. Simply stating that you are willing to do anything is not sufficient. It is important to weigh all the factors about yourself. Consider these important questions: What kind of job do you want? Why do you want it? How do you qualify for it?

The Importance of Character and Attitude

Although specialized knowledge and skills are the major requisites for some jobs, many personnel experts put 75 to 85 percent of their emphasis on personal qualifications, appearance, character, intelligence, dependability, and attitude. Experience at a particular level is valuable, but it cannot substitute for honesty, the ability to work and get along with others, resourcefulness, and initiative. Many persons who are experts in their fields fail to advance because they lack one or more of these traits. Employers are also keenly interested in how you measure up to their corporate image.

Appearance

Employers are also sensitive to the personal appearance of job applicants. Neatness and cleanliness not only count, but they count for a lot. A disheveled, unkempt appearance may be read as a sign of sloppiness or irresponsibility. You have only one or two opportunities while you are being interviewed to make a good impression, so be sure your clothes and personal grooming are working for you.

Choosing a Direction

An important step in looking for a job is to ascertain where the jobs are likely to be, how you are qualified for them (or what you can do to make yourself qualified), and how you can ferret out these jobs. Anyone embarking on a major job hunt needs to have more than a nodding acquaintance with the job market generally and the employment opportunities open to them specifically.

Employment Opportunities in the U.S.

Opportunities for employment in the United States fall into three general categories: goods-producing, such as farming, mining, manufacturing, and construction; services-producing, such as health and education, clerical, and management; and government agencies, which are a combination of the goods-producing and services-producing categories.

The Employment Outlook

Most persons work in the services-producing sector; the goods-producing sector, in fact, employs only about one-third of the nation's work force. Through the mid-1980s, employment in the services sector is expected to increase more rapidly than in the goods-producing sector. Subdivisions in each of the three general areas, however, will show varied expansion, depending upon individual need. For example, while the need for farmers is expected to decrease in coming years, there will be specialized areas of farming where the need for workers will continue to grow.

Account must also be taken of general and specific business trends. A move that leads to attrition in one specific area may also open the way for new jobs in a related area. The trend toward conglomeration, for example, will contribute to reduced numbers of persons working in middle management and increased numbers working with computers and in other technical jobs. Jobs, in general, will become more complex and specialized in the 1980s, a condition that results in a greater number of overall career choices.

Among the broad occupational groups, white-collar jobs have increased most rapidly in recent years. In the late-1970s there were almost 12 million more white-collar workers—professional, managerial, clerical, and sales—than those classified as blue-collar—craftsmen, operators, and laborers. Through the mid-1980s, continued growth is expected in white-collar and service occupations, while opportunities for blue-collar and farm workers will decline.

Demand will continue to grow for personnel in research and development, education and health, and in all segments of clerical work.

Overall, the number of managers will increase about as fast as the average for other occupations. Business organizations and government agencies will continue to require managers and administrators in order to function efficiently. And a large proportion of self-employed managers will retire or seek other roles as the trend toward larger corporations restricts the total number of small businesses and as supermarkets and other large stores displace small groceries and general stores.

Skilled job seekers will find employment opportunities in the years ahead. Because of the complex nature of many jobs, employers will require staffs with increasingly higher levels of education. Employment in clerical, professional, and technical fields will grow faster than in all other occupational areas.

Choosing a Field

Assume that you are about to embark on a job hunt. You have a general idea of your career preference. You have probably spent from one to six years studying your field or gaining practical experience in it. Perhaps you have acquired the basic fundamentals in export traffic, market conditions, and diplomatic techniques that are necessary to a foreign relations officer. Or if you have studied the principles of advertising and news gathering you may hope to enter the field of public relations. An acquaintance with employment procedures, labor relations problems, and systems of job evaluation would equip you for a position in personnel management.

Whatever your area of specialization, the first step is to survey your chosen field and ask yourself: Where are the best opportunities? What phases of the work am I most qualified to handle?

There are several ways to answer these questions. Having some actual experience helps. After a brief period on the job, you should be able to determine whether you are truly fitted by temperament and training to fill your responsibilities successfully. You may discover that the environment is not to your liking, or that the demands of the work are greater than you thought. You can also talk with faculty members or occupational consultants who are familiar with your vocational ambitions and the field you seek to enter. Then, too, seek advice from people already working in the career that appeals to you. Business or professional leaders who understand your strong and weak points may be able to steer you in the correct direction. Consult a placement director who is in touch with employment opportunities in your field. He may be able to point out what kinds of openings best suit your present ability and experience. Finally, if you are one of the many persons with broad interests and general qualifications, aptitude tests or personal interviews with vocational guidance experts may help you decide how best to use your talents. Be sure that your test is administered by an organization approved by the National Vocational Guidance Association. Do not be lured into paying large fees for tests by unreliable organizations.

When the career you desire requires more training than you possess, make up your deficiencies by attending night school classes or by taking correspondence courses in related areas. Another alternative is to enroll in a school or college offering a cooperative program, so you can study part time and work part time in the field you hope to enter. In any case, concentrate on obtaining the expertise needed to fill the job you want. Nothing is more frustrating than to be hired for a desirable job, only to discover that you are unable to perform your duties successfully.

You may want to narrow your scope and specialize in a particular aspect of a broad field. Specialization can pay high financial dividends. It is also beneficial in case of emergency to possess a variety of vocational skills. For example, during an economic slump or depression, a person who can type or take dictation or work at a craft may be able to support himself on the basis of these skills alone.

Choosing a career is really a matter of learning what you want to do. Collect as much data about a field as you can through personal contact with persons already working in the field, professional publications, employment counselors, and, if possible, some firsthand experience. Once you have settled on a field, set a goal and work toward it at all times and by all means. At the same time, be prepared for any eventuality by developing more than one skill.

When You Begin to Look for a Position

If you are not working, you can easily conduct an all-out, no-holds-barred job search. If you are still employed, however, you need a discreet—if not downright secret—strategy for two reasons. First, your present employers are likely to resent the fact that you are about to desert the team, and you could be placing your present job in jeopardy. Second, when another company is considering hiring you, it may be for a job where the incumbent does not know he is about to be replaced—and any premature announcements on your part could still put the job in jeopardy for you.

However you go about a job search, you need to command every possible resource. The sections that follow describe all the possible sources for help in job hunting.

Private Executive Recruiters, Counselors, and Agencies

Generally, three kinds of private businesses or agencies can help in your job search: executive recruiters, who are the elite of employment agencies; general private employment agencies, not as elite but very time-tested when it comes to placing persons in middle-management jobs that consultants often do not handle; and job counselors, who help you prepare for the job hunt and who may or may not actually have contacts with potential employers.

Payment to consultants and private employment agencies is a matter of custom and/or law; sometimes the employer pays the fee and sometimes the new employee does. Job counselors always expect you to pay, regardless of whether or not they actually place you.

Executive Recruiters

These employment agents, often referred to as headhunters, work only in the top levels of business. They maintain tight, close ties with the corporations whom they represent. Their job is to recruit prospective employees for their clients—they may even approach you when you are seemingly happily employed.

Consultants check out your references and do all necessary preliminary screening before they present you to their client.

More and more organizations are taking personality into consideration. They are no longer interested solely in scholastic achievement or previous work experience. They want to know about your alertness, manners, ability to get along with people, punctuality, respect for authority, and reliability.

Health

General good health is also essential to performance in any activity. All jobs make some physical demands on the worker. Many companies require new employees to pass physical examinations to determine whether they are physically able to carry out their duties. Make certain that you can meet the physical requirements of the position you want.

Executive Job Counselors

These persons help you prepare a resume and counsel you about the type of work for which you are most suited. Rather than putting you in touch with companies that have definite openings, they are more likely to provide you with a list of potential employers so you can do a mass mailing, or they may provide the mailing as one of their services.

Often you can do for yourself what these companies do for you, but if you are not a self-motivated person, these companies may supply a needed push.

Employment Agencies

Private agencies act as intermediaries between employers and job seekers. They offer diversified opportunities and a wide circle of contacts. They have frequently built up friendly relations with personnel directors at major corporations and are able to obtain entry into companies where positions are hard to get.

From the point of view of the employer, an agency sells the advantages of the company to a prospective employee and often works to overcome such objections as "the location is inconvenient," "working conditions don't seem just right," or "the hours don't appeal to me."

Employment agencies are regulated by state or local authorities. Any introduction to a prospective employer, therefore, may be accepted with confidence.

Placement agency personnel are skilled in detecting the abilities and talents and exploring the personalities of candidates, and their screening techniques provide a reliable evaluation. They also work to match employers and employees. The agency may know that the vice-president who needs an assistant has a difficult temper and requires a mature, tranquil individual in order to work harmoniously with him.

State Employment Services

Each state has an employment service with offices in principal communities. Perhaps you are already acquainted with the employment service through local advertising. Whether you live in a large city or a small town, your local employment service offers help in obtaining a job, counsels about the kind of job that best suits you, and provides information about training opportunities. No fee is charged for these services. If there is no state employment service office in your community, write to the headquarters in the state capital to find out where the nearest local office is or whether part-time service is provided to your community.

The Business Pages of Newspapers and Journals

Although the help-wanted ads are a source of information that almost no one overlooks, few persons keep as close an eye as they might on the business news in their field. It offers many clues to job possibilities.

Clip out and save articles about the opening of new plants or offices, the expansion of corporations, department stores, and manufacturing facilities here and abroad, and the development of new products. Usually, these stories indicate an increase or change in personnel. Contact the personnel manager of the company you are interested in to ask about the new opportunities for employment in his company.

Also, a personal item about the promotion, transfer, or resignation of an employee may reveal a vacancy for which you are qualified. Follow up such a lead.

Help-Wanted Advertisements

Help-wanted classified and display advertisements appear regularly in newspapers and in specialized weekly and monthly magazines. They fall into two categories: the open ad, which identifies the name of the company and its address, and the blind ad, which provides only a box number to which the applicant must write. It is usually preferable to answer an open ad because you know the company's name, its location, and possibly something about its business, reputation, and dependability. The blind ad is used by firms that may not want to reveal that they need new employees—such a public announcement could have a disturbing effect on present employees. You have less chance of obtaining a response from a blind ad than from an open ad.

Do not be taken in by glowingly worded ads. They are often written merely to entice good applicants to a position under false pretenses. Beware of ads that ask you to take a course, deposit money, or buy samples, as these are often disguised ways of selling something presented in the form of job opportunities.

Friends and Acquaintances

It is often said that "It's not what you know, but whom you know" that helps you obtain a good position. In many instances, this is undoubtedly true, and it is indeed unfortunate when a less qualified person is given preference for a position over someone far better qualified simply because of the influence of a friend in a key spot. And, obviously, you cannot depend on clout to secure employment. Still, do not overlook friends who may be of real assistance. If you inform an employed friend of your abilities and experience, he may know of a vacancy in his company or elsewhere for which you are ideally suited. Salespersons are in a particularly good position to help; they are in constant touch with employers and may learn of openings before they are turned over to agencies or advertised in newspapers.

There is one note of caution: Do not pester your friends about jobs. Simply let them know of your availability and what you can do. Do ask them to help you. Most persons appreciate your problem because they have at one time been in your position, and they may help you in every possible way. But if you tend to use your friends or hound them, they will not cooperate and will even begin to avoid you. Through your own poor judgment, you may lose a good opportunity and antagonize your friends as well.

Registry Services

Personnel consultants and college placement offices often run registry services that send bulletins either gratis or on a subscription basis to large companies. In some instances, companies pay a flat fee to receive regular bulletins announcing the availability of professionals and high-level executives. In other cases, they pay for the registry plus a percentage of the first year's salary of the employee engaged through this method.

It may be worth your while to submit your application to a registry service. When calls are received for executive jobs, the registry service matches the resume of the applicant with available positions on file. The applicant is notified, and arrangements are made for an interview. You can also specify which companies you do not want your application sent to.

Preparing to Look for a Job: A Summary

Once you have completed training for the type of work you are seeking and have mentally or otherwise reviewed your capacities, there are several steps to conducting a systematic job hunt. These are:

1. Take stock of yourself. Prepare a written dossier listing your skills and responsibilities on present and past jobs, as well as your likes and dislikes with regard to work tasks.
2. Appraise the various job requirements for the kind of work you hope to obtain. Draw up a chart showing how your skills and talents match the requirements.
3. Contact all your job sources—employment agencies, personal contacts, trade journals, and business directories. Don't forget to watch the help-wanted columns of the newspapers.
4. Prepare a resume that will serve as your basic resume and from which you can write specialized resumes as individual job possibilities require.
5. When you find a job you wish to apply for, write a cover letter geared specifically to that job. Enclose it with a copy of your resume.
6. Begin to prepare for the interview. Do homework on the company and talk with any contacts who may be able to give you more information on the company. Interviews are often set up on short notice, but if you have done your preparatory work, you will be prepared when the big opportunity presents itself.

2

Choosing the Best
Resume Format

THERE ARE A NUMBER OF resume styles and formats in use today. The kind that you choose to write depends on which aspect of yourself and your work experience you want to draw attention to. Any person can use any of the following resume styles, but you will want to choose one that most clearly states what your experience and hopes for future work are.

The styles of resumes in common use today are the basic resume, the chronological resume, the functional resume, and the modern analytical resume.

The basic resume is best suited for a new graduate or for someone seeking a job in a skilled or technical area.

The chronological resume is well suited to persons in publishing, advertising, and other areas of communication. It also works well for persons in retailing, and for anyone who has held many different jobs.

The functional resume is widely used in business and the professions. It can be helpful if you are planning to change fields.

The modern analytical resume works well for anyone willing to take the time to develop it. It is the *crème de la crème* of resumes; it takes more work and time to prepare, but it is well worth the effort, especially if you are seeking a high-powered position and want to present your skills and capabilities in the best possible light. Not every person will require so definitive a resume as the modern analytical resume, but no one will be hurt by using it.

The sections that follow contain more information and models of each type of resume.

Preparing a Basic Resume

If you think you do not need a written resume, if you are a skilled worker, or if you are a new graduate seeking your first job, then the basic resume is probably best for your needs. Almost everyone enhances his prospects for employment if he is organized enough to put something about himself in writing, and this is the primary function of the basic resume.

Basic resumes usually consist of two sections:

1. Introductory information: your name, address, telephone number, and any personal information or interests you wish to include.
2. Several paragraphs describing your work experience and your education or vocational training.

Evaluate yourself fairly in a basic resume, but do not be afraid to brag a little about special achievements, work projects, or academic honors. Some basic resumes also include a list of personal characteris tics (e.g., energetic, willing to learn new material) that demonstrate your willingness to work.

If the kind of work you do requires a license, you should describe the kind you have. For example: "I have a license that qualifies me as a master plumber in New York State, Illinois, and the District of Columbia."

You might be willing to accept a position that someone else finds undesirable, and this should be noted on the resume. For example, a job might call for evening hours or for working weekends; it might be in a neighborhood that many would find undesirable; or it might be too far from home. If you are willing to overlook such objectional aspects of a job, an employer might be more inclined to hire you.

Special Advice for the New Graduate

The basic resume is perfect for your needs because it allows you to play up experiences that are related to the type of position you are seeking. List any part-time work done during school vacations or the school year if you worked while attending school. You might describe school subjects that relate directly to the type of work you hope to obtain. Include in this material any details and dates of your education, any special skills acquired in volunteer work, and anything you feel you have learned through the pursuit of hobbies and special interests. Particularly on a first job, any special skills you have acquired through serious pursuit of hobbies or special interests can be a stepping-stone to a full-time position.

Preparing a Chronological Resume

The chief advantage of a chronological resume is that it enables you to list and yet play down jobs that may have little relevance to the type of work you are now seeking. Furthermore, many of your past jobs may not be representative of your present ability, yet to omit them on a resume would be to leave unexplained gaps in time. A chronological resume permits you to list every job you have ever held, while allotting greater time and detail to the more recently held jobs that will relate directly to the type of work you hope to do.

A chronological resume is ideal for someone who has held many different jobs; persons in publishing and other areas of communication and retailing often use this type of resume for this very reason.

The chronological resume is best described as an experience record that includes brief job descriptions. If you have held a number of jobs, you may be wasting valuable time and space listing work that is not related to the job you now hope to obtain. Furthermore, some of your past job experiences may be below your present level of ability, and there is no point in describing jobs like these in the same detail you would use for more recent, relevant jobs.

The most accepted organization of a chronological resume is as follows:

1. Name, address, and telephone number.
2. Age; marital status; military standing; willingness to travel or relocate, if applicable; and any other personal information.
3. Educational experience. List schools attended, degrees received, and years of attendance, beginning with the most recent.
4. Work experience. List in chronological order, beginning with your most recent experience. State the name of the company, the position you held there, the years of employment, and then write a brief paragraph or more describing your work experiences and responsibilities. If several early jobs are totally irrelevant except to explain a gap in time, skip the descriptive paragraphs for these categories.
5. References. Simply note that your references are available on request. References are never listed directly on a resume, but you should be prepared with the names of two or three colleagues or superiors who will vouch for the quality of your work. Personal references are never given, unless specifically requested.

The title of a chronological resume should reflect the level of the job you hope to obtain. If this is not possible, you may list a brief objective stating the kind of work you are seeking, as is done in the model.

Other categories that are sometimes added to a chronological resume include scholastic honors (for new graduates only) and professional memberships. You may include a desired salary range or the statement that "Salary is open to negotiation," but since these statements do not really tell a prospective employer anything definite, they are more often than not omitted from resumes these days.

Model Basic Resume

WELDER

May 19—

Leslie J. Engle
770 Missouri Boulevard
Los Angeles, CA 90017
Telephone: (213)877-4302

Good health
Willing to relocate
Will work in any section of city

Learned welding in technical school and then spent several years in on-the-job training. Became a skilled manual arc and gas welder and combination welder. Have knowledge of blueprint reading, welding symbols, metal properties, and electricity. Possess manual dexterity, good eyesight, and excellent eye-hand coordination.

During the last four years, I have worked on the construction of bridges, building steel structures and storage tanks. I worked from plans, drawings, blueprints, written specifications, and determined the proper sequence of operations for each job.

I have supervised teams of five to ten persons.

ELECTRONICS TECHNICIAN

January 19—

William H. Strand
25 Jackson Street
Little Falls, NJ 07424   Telephone: (201) 697-4777

Born: 5/7/55
Excellent health
Willing to relocate

Studied electronics in the U.S. Army Specialized School for Electronics. My first assignment was as an assembler. Discharged with rank of master sergeant.

My position in the army can be described as that of electronics technician. I was in charge of planning and coordinating the flow of work through the shop. I reported trouble spots to the supervising officer. I also maintained and repaired all electronics equipment at stations, including radio and radar equipment used for communications, detection, ranging, recognition, and countermeasures. I learned to use the tools and testing devices commonly employed in electronics service work, as well as how to calibrate, tune, and adjust equipment.

I am a high school graduate. I participated in a two-year (1974-76) electronics course at Steinmetz Vocational High School, Schenectady, New York.

Model Chronological Resume

LIBRARIAN

2/20/—

Ruth A. Roe
487 Franklin Drive
Woodland, NY 10124
(213) 561-2573

Marital status: Married, no children. Born in New York City.
Date of birth: October 1942

Employment Objective

Position as children's librarian

Education

Columbia University, New York, New York, M.L.S. in Library
Science, 1969.
Hunter College, New York, New York, B.S., 1964. Major:
Elementary Education. Minor: Child Psychology

Experience

1964-68. Woodland Elementary School, 231 Ritchie Lane,
Woodland, New York. Teacher of fifth grade. A major
objective was to stimulate pupils to do more independent
reading. To this end, prepared displays and organized
field trips to nearby libraries in connection with annual
book fair; assisted part-time librarian in reorganizing
instructional materials center to make it easier to use
and more inviting in appearance; took training courses;
and for two years, conducted a junior great-books course
for pupils at Woodland.

1963-64. Part time during school year and full time during summer of 1964. Bowen Library, 441 Playford Street, New York, New York. Library clerk. Located books for patrons and answered nonprofessional inquiries. Received, sorted, repaired, and shelved books.

Summer 1963. Mobile Manufacturing Company, 24 West Fifth Street, Woodland, New York. Clerk-typist. Acted as secretary to vice-president while regular secretary was on vacation.

Summer 1961 and 1962. Highpoint Camp, Wilson Road, Adirondack, New York. Counselor. Taught arts and crafts and supervised bunk of ten- and eleven-year-old girls.

Special Skills

Spanish: Good reading, writing, and speaking knowledge. Can operate various types of audiovisual equipment.

References

Available on request.

Preparing the Functional Resume

A functional resume is organized according to functional areas of experience. Some personnel advisers consider it the most basic and useful of all resumes. In analyzing your work history for a functional resume, you disclose your assets in such a way that they point directly to the job you are seeking.

Select only those items from your experience that relate to the job you seek. Omit any irrelevant details. At best, these details might provide interesting background, but if you have held a number of jobs, you may only be using valuable space by including information that does not serve your immediate purpose.

Concentrate on how the kinds of jobs you have held relate to the kind of job you want. For example, if you are a technician, you might arrange your functional resume according to the projects you worked on, presenting each in problem-solving form. If you are a copywriter, you might base your functional resume on the different kinds of copy you wrote, the various media you wrote for, or the different products you were concerned with.

Organize your experience so it demonstrates how you have the qualifications for the job you want. Begin by working with two lists: one describing the functions of the job you want, and the other, your job history. Match each job description on your worksheet with a corresponding function of the prospective job. If you are qualified for a job, you will begin to discover how the functions of the prospective job are similar to those of other jobs you have held.

A functional resume also brings to light "hidden" experience that you can apply to a new field if you are attempting to switch fields. For example, suppose you are applying for an accounting position and you have previously worked as a clerk; you need to identify any duties you had as a clerk that are applicable to the field of accounting. You may have kept records on one job, checked record entries on another, and worked as an accounting assistant on a third job. All these experiences can be applied to the field of accounting, and in a correctly written functional resume, this "hidden" accounting experience becomes apparent.

A functional resume is organized in the following way:

1. Name, address, and telephone number.
2. Areas of experience. Break these down into skills, areas of responsibility or expertise, or knowledge areas—whatever works well for you. Follow each category head with a brief paragraph describing your skills and abilities in that area.
3. Employment record. This is where you list specifically the names of companies that have employed you, the dates of your employment, and your titles.

Model Functional Resume

TECHNICAL WRITER

Pamela Barry
6 West Fifty-sixth Street
New York, NY 10019
Telephone: (212) 457-9907

Areas of Experience

Technical writing. My specialty is taking the material and research of scientists, engineers, and other technical specialists and writing it in a format acceptable to the average consumer. Presenting products that meet with consumer resistance is another area of specialization, as is developing new-product information.

Research. I am capable and experienced in studying reports, reading technical reports, and interviewing technical and scientific personnel to obtain the information I need for writing assignments.

Production. I am a skilled photo researcher, can write copy to fit and can spec type, and am able to follow a writing project through all stages of production. I have supervised layout and keyline personnel.

Employment Record

1970 to present	Grow Chemical Company, New York, New York. Technical writer.
1964–1970	Hamilton Richfield Corporation, New York, New York. Technical advertising writer.

Education

1965–   M.A. in Communications, Columbia University
1966   (night school), New York, New York.

1960–   B.S. in Engineering, with honors, Princeton
1964   University, Princeton, New Jersey.

Professional Affiliations

Society of Technical Writers and Publishers
American Society of Mechanical Engineers
National Association of Science Writers

Personal Data

Willing to relocate
Willing to travel

References

Available on request

4. Professional affiliations, if any. List the groups to which you belong and any positions of responsibility you have held with them.
5. Personal information. If you wish, you can include this category, mentioning age, marital status, willingness to travel or relocate.
6. References. Do not forget to add a reference statement.

Preparing the Modern Analytical Resume

Most of the model resumes in this book follow this format. The modern analytical resume, also known as the target resume or the analytical resume, is an excellent selling tool for executives. It clearly explains your job objective, offers a summary of your experience, and then presents your experience in more detailed form. This resume is designed to grab the attention of the reader initially and then make him want to continue reading. The modern analytical resume is widely accepted by personnel executives within major corporations and by executive recruiters.

This resume should be organized in the following way:

1. Name, address, and telephone number.
2. Summary of work experience. This generally consists of one to three paragraphs describing your strong points and your major areas of responsibilities and experience. Whenever possible, this should be written to meet the expectations of the person for whom you hope to work. For example, if you are seeking a position as controller for a manufacturing company, the summary of experience should play up any elements from your past work experience that will show how you are qualified for the controller's position. The summary of your work experience has one purpose: to grab the reader and convince him that you are the person he is seeking.
3. Occupational objective. This should be a short description of the kind of position you are looking for. You may, if you wish, add any qualifiers such as "middle-sized hospital," "manufacturing firm," "services-oriented corporation," or "urban location." A single sentence or a very short paragraph is sufficient for a job objective.
4. Work record. In this section, you list your past work experiences, including the names of the companies, the titles you held, and the years you were employed at each. Begin with your most recent position.
5. List the schools attended, years attended, degrees awarded, and major and minor areas of specialization, if pertinent.
6. Professional affiliations. List any groups to which you belong and offices or honors related to them.
7. Personal data. At a minimum, you should note that you are willing to

relocate and travel, if you are. If you are not, omit any reference to the fact. Beyond this, you may want to add your marital status, age, the fact that your health is excellent, and any other information that may be relevant.

8. References. Add a statement noting that your references are available on request.

Several optional categories can also be added to the modern analytical resume. These include knowledge of a foreign language, if pertinent, and military service, which should always be added to account for any gaps in time. Early background (where you went to school before college, when you lived outside the U.S., your parents' backgrounds or nationalities, etc.) and outside activities should be mentioned only if you think they will be of interest to the person interviewing you. Generally, such information is best brought out during an interview.

The main reason for preparing a resume is to display your experience, background, and training to a prospective employer so that he can judge whether your capabilities will contribute to the success of his organization. Preparing a resume effectively is no easy trick. The art of resume writing is probably the least understood of all forms of business communication. It is not taught in schools. Top copywriters, adept at promoting everything from undeveloped arid land to collapsible toothbrushes, find themselves stymied when they try to sell themselves through a resume. Even highly qualified executives continue to approach resume preparation halfheartedly.

The first step in resume preparation is to consider what a resume is and what it is not. A resume is not an autobiography. Nor is it your personal memoir. It is an advertisement of yourself. The facts selected for use in a resume should emphasize your accomplishments and abilities, but they should not tell everything about you. All the resume can do is get you invited for an interview. During the interview, you can offer any details appropriate to the position you seek.

Model Modern Analytical Resume

CORPORATE CONTROLLER

Resume of   Joseph F. Fenton
345 Verrazano Avenue
Brookline, MA 02187   Telephone: (617)976-9482

Summary of
Experience   Over sixteen years of solid experience in corporate accounting management, design of cost systems, and budgets; experience in SEC and public reporting. Proven ability to work effectively with line and senior management.

Occupational
Objective   Position with a corporation where my knowledge of accounting and financial statements and ability to perform as a shirt-sleeve executive is appropriately remunerated.

Work Record
Fullerton Investments, Inc.
Boston, Massachusetts

1970 to
present   **Financial Management Assistant to the President.** I specialize in financial management decisions regarding

* municipal bonds and revenue issues,
* dispositions and exchanges or additions to
   the company's portfolios,
* credit analysis of financial statements and
   operations.

Federated Operations, Inc.
Morristown, New Jersey

1966 to
1970   **Accounting Systems Analyst.** Responsibilities with this firm included interviews at all management levels to determine the requirements for systems development or modification for the accounting efficiency of each department or division. Dealt with various data processing systems. Was a key member of the management team of this corporation.
Other responsibilities included

* performing internal audit functions,
* compiling consolidated monthly financial reports,
* coordinating divisional budgets,
* supervising cash control,
* developing profit improvement projects,
* assisting in acquisition analysis.

Page 1 of 2

<u>Havemeyer Industries, Inc.</u>
New York, New York

1963 to   <u>Assistant to the Corporate Controller.</u> My duties with this
1966   multinational commodity trading company included

                 * assisting in development of accounting systems
                    and procedures for EDP,
                 * supervising the preparation of financial
                    statements and reports involving domestic
                    and foreign subsidiaries,
                 * directing the accounting staff.

                 This position required exceptional communications
                 skills.

<u>Educational</u>   B.S. in Industrial Management, Massachusetts Institute of
<u>Background</u>   Technology, June 1963. Emphasis on analysis of business
                 problems and understanding managerial principles.
                 Included use of many rapidly developing mathematical and
                 statistical techniques for solving industrial problems,
                 with training in programming techniques. Senior thesis:
                 "Programming in Business Management." Ranked in upper
                 sixth in graduating class of 150. Elected to Phi Beta
                 Kappa.

<u>Military</u>   U.S. Army. Served eighteen months in West Germany.
<u>Service</u>   Honorably discharged with the rank of sergeant in 1959.

<u>Professional</u>   Data Processing Management Association
<u>Affiliations</u>   Association for Computing

<u>Outside</u>   Member of local political club. Active in community
<u>Activities</u>   welfare organizations.

<u>Personal Data</u>   Born February 10, 1940, Jamaica, New York. Willing to
                 relocate.

<u>References</u>   References available on request.

Choosing the Best Resume Format **23**

3

Preparing
an Effective Resume

Many otherwise self-confident executives are at a loss as to how to present themselves most effectively in a resume when faced with an immediate job search. Perhaps this quandary is related to the reason for the job search—you may have been reorganized out of a job; you may have been fired; or someone in your family may be ill, necessitating a move to a new region. Unfortunately, writing a resume is often the first step most persons take after losing or giving up a job. Yet it is important not to let your mood or temporary feelings of discouragement about yourself spill over to your resume. Remember that the reason for leaving one job, as well as the reason for seeking another job, should never appear on your resume.

One way to avoid ever having to prepare a resume at a time when you feel less than self-confident is to maintain a dossier on yourself. The dossier should contain all the pertinent information, including the details of your present employment, that is needed to convert it to a resume format should the need arise.

Many persons consider the preparation of such a personal inventory a waste of time. They are happily employed with no thoughts of repositioning. Yet, maintaining a personal inventory permits you to be prepared for an opportunity that may suddenly arise—and it saves you from ever having to do the nitty-gritty work of preparing a resume at a time when you lack confidence. Here is a breakdown of the categories of information you should maintain in your dossier. These same categories also appear on resumes, although every category may not be applicable to every resume.

1. **Name, address, and telephone number.**

2. **Summary of experience.** In about fifty words, more if you have

considerable experience, summarize the duties and responsibilities you have assumed in the positions you have held up to the present.

3. **Occupational Objective.** The objective is a short description of your occupational goal. Include only the salient points of the position you desire.

4. **Work record.** List all positions, including your present one, and give concise information about your responsibilities and length of experience. Begin by writing this information on separate sheets of paper. Next, extract the most important material and edit it into resume format. Do not be afraid to blow your horn; this section should look like an advertisement for you. On the other hand, do not fool yourself about your skills; be honest with yourself. List the jobs that you do well, such as auditor, bookkeeper, or statistician. If you are a graduate of a business administration course, you may be equipped to hold a position in an accounting department or in a statistical division—this is the time to consider all possible directions.

5. **Education.** Give details of any special training you have had. Name institutions where you have studied and dates of attendance. This record must be clear because many firms require a full chronological description of your education and degrees. Indicate your major and minor disciplines. Mention any special courses taken, whether single subjects or a complete program of study, that might help you get a job.

6. **Professional affiliations and licenses.** Information about membership in professional societies can be presented on a resume. State any title or administrative post you now hold or have held and whether you are an active, honorary, professional, or lay member. If your work requires licensing from local, state, or federal authorities, or a private group, name each license you hold and the group or agency that grants it.

7. **Personal recognition.** State the titles, publishers, and dates of all pertinent printed articles, papers, theses, or books you have written. If your profession is one in which "literary visibility" is valued, make the list as complete as possible; otherwise, you need present only a few key publications. Note similar recognition in scientific, technical, or political fields.

8. **Clubs and fraternities.** Enumerate the names of any political, social, religious, civic, and community organizations in which you participate actively. This information reflects something about you personally. This section is optional.

9. **Knowledge of foreign languages.** Mention any knowledge of foreign languages. Those whose duties may involve travel abroad are better equipped for such assignments if they are able to communicate with business persons overseas in their native tongue.

10. **Personal interests and hobbies.** You may want to list one or two avocations or interests that you enjoy and follow in your free time. Emphasize any that are directly related to your career. Also include any clubs or societies related to your hobby to which you belong. This section is optional, although questions on personal interests are found on virtually all application blanks.

11. **Personal data.** This entry could include any of the following data, although all these items are optional: date of birth, birthplace, marital status, number of children, height, weight, and state of health.
    If you have traveled, briefly state where and when. Also, note if you are willing to relocate.

12. **Salary.** Although you can indicate your salary range, this is often omitted. You should certainly wait to discuss a specific figure until you are granted an interview.

13. **References.** These should not be quoted, but your resume should note that they are available on request. Collect letters of recommendation from past employers and prominent individuals who know you well. Have duplicates made so that you will not have to give out the originals. Alternately, you can supply the names, addresses, and telephone numbers of three or four persons who can vouch for your professional capabilities.

14. **Date.** Put the year the resume was written in the lower right-hand corner of the last page.

15. **Pagination.** If your resume is more than one page long, type at the bottom of each page: "Page 1 of 2," or "Page 2 of 2," depending on the total number of pages in your resume. A prospective employer can then easily check the length of your resume. If the pages become separated on his desk, he can also immediately determine how many pages he should have. At the top of pages 2 and 3, write "Resume of (your name)," and the word "Continued."

Based on the categories just described, here is a model resume:

GEOLOGICAL ENGINEER

Resume of
(1)

James V. Thompson
5420 Buckeye Avenue East
Spokane, WA 99207   Telephone (509) 678-9023

Summary of
Experience
(2)

Twenty years of experience collecting geological data
used by government agencies and private industry. Supervised test drilling programs for petroleum exploration.
Interpreted data assembled in geological surveys for
further analysis by engineers and technical personnel.
Determined geological formations related to ground water
conditions.

Occupational
Objective
(3)

To be associated with a firm or agency that will fully
utilize my geological engineering background and provide
an opportunity for continued achievement so that I may
contribute to the advancement of my field, whether in a
public or private capacity.

Work
Record
(4)
1970 to
present

United States Geological Survey
Spokane, Washington

Geologist. Prepare and maintain plans for engineering
geology branch of Geological Survey in Pacific Northwest;
make all public and official contacts required; provide
the basic geologic data necessary in national program of
resource development for power, navigation, irrigation,
flood control, and industrial expansion. Organize geological engineering programs and projects.

Research investigations of landslides along upper Columbia River valley in state of Washington. Devise new
methods of studying landslides. Have classified more than
300 landslides for statistical analysis of slide factors
in evaluating environmental geologic relationships.
Study comparisons of slide and nonslide slopes to appraise
relative stability of natural slopes. Coordinate field
and office work, write and supervise preparation of maps
and reports, select and assign personnel.

United States Bureau of Reclamation
Grand Coulee Dam, Washington

1965 to
1970

Project Geologist. Worked in concrete control section,
making mix analyses, gravel gradings, sand gradings,
moisture determinations, and silt tests. Also made X-ray
inspections, kept strain-gauge records, and inspected
stress-relief welding.

Page 1 of 2
(15)

Preparing an Effective Resume **27**

Formulated test drilling program. Supervised exploration
drilling. Conducted investigations, prepared and interpreted data for use of designers and engineers. Determined
geological formations, the related groundwater conditions, and the interpretation of these data as they
influenced engineering problems. Investigated structural relationships on basalt terrain and effects on
engineering developments.

Prepared maps, drawings, and charts to illustrate features studied. Selected staff personnel.

                      Demosthenes Oil Company
                        Sinclair, Wyoming

1960 to   Geological Engineer. Participated in foundation tests.
1965   Inspected excavations. Member of field-engineering con-
               struction team for a cracking plant. Worked on housing
               program to rebuild 275 homes and business buildings.
               Inspected pressure vessels. Did geological mapping of
               mines and claims; did engineering work related to mapping
               and mining operations at Alma and Fairplay, Colorado.

Education   Colorado School of Mines, Golden, Colorado. B.S. in
(5)   Geological Engineering, June 1960. Followed regular
               curriculum, with extra courses in petroleum and petroleum
               refining. Active in intramural basketball, skiing.
               Elected to Tau Beta Pi. Expenses financed with part-time
               employment and family funds.

Scientific   Northwest Scientific Association
Affiliations   Geological Society of America
(6)
Personal
Recognition   Listing in American Men of Science, 1970.
(7)
Personal   Follow professional football and baseball. Member of the
Interests   Northwest Engineers Bowling Team.
(10)

Personal Data Born 3/26/38.
(11)   Married, two children.

Salary   In the range of $30,000.
(12)

References   Available on request.
(13)

28 EFFECTIVE RESUMES FOR EXECUTIVES AND SPECIALIZED PERSONNEL

Using the Model Resumes

The resumes that appear later in this book are organized by job classification. Model yours after the ones that approximate your experience and qualifications. Be sure that your resume follows the models in appearance and length, and that it is well organized.

Format of a Resume

A resume should be as neatly typed and as well organized as possible. It should be typed on white or off-white paper, 8½ by 11 inches in size. Odd sizes, such as legal paper or small stationery paper, are difficult to file and easily lost, once filed.

Length of Resume

While brevity is important, professional persons and executives usually have extensive and solid experience, which may take several pages to detail. Try not to go over three pages, however, because employers seldom have time to read more than this. Furthermore, anything longer than three pages indicates lack of planning and organizational skills and a disregard of the traditional resume length, two faults which may displease a prospective employer or a personnel recruiter.

Revealing Race and Age on a Resume

It is customary but not necessary to state your age on a resume. You may also state your race. Remember, though, that according to the Fair Employment Practice laws in many states, a job applicant cannot be compelled to reveal age, ancestry, national origin, race, or religion, so you can feel fairly safe in omitting any one of these details if you so choose.

Using Good English

Your resume should be written in the best English you can muster. If this is a weak area for you, have someone who knows grammar check over your resume carefully before you retype it in final form.

When describing your present job, use the present tense if you like; or, write your entire resume in the past tense. For example: "Direct research program" or "Administered training program."

Final Resume Preparations

When your resume is ready to go, there are a few finishing touches that show you know the ropes of job hunting. Most professional resumes are enclosed in a special folder known as a "blue backer." This type of binder is preferred over stiff covers that never seem to fit a manila envelope properly and which add unnecessary weight when the resume is mailed to prospective employers. Blue backers are available in stationery stores.

Enclosing a Cover Letter

After completing your resume, you must also write a cover letter. Usually, a cover letter indicates when you will be available for an interview and for employment. You should ask for an interview in a cover letter and possibly point out why you think you are suited for the job you seek. A cover letter should never be longer than one page. You can write a general cover letter of the type that you might enclose in a mass mailing, or you can write individual cover letters geared to the specific job you are seeking. The latter is preferred in most instances.

What to Avoid on a Resume

- Photographs are generally not sent once you have reached the executive level. The only purpose in enclosing one is to strengthen your identification and to help distinguish your application from others. In most states, a prospective employer may not request a photo from a prospective employee. If you have strong feelings about enclosing a photo, you may, of course, do so, but it is not particularly recommended.
- Do not use abbreviations, with the exception of titles, corporate or company names, and states. If you use a state abbreviation, a period is used after the traditional abbreviation but the period is omitted after the new post office–issued abbreviations such as IL for Illinois and WA for Washington. (See appendix.)
- Do not state a specific salary requirement; leave yourself room for negotiation during an interview.
- Do not send carbon copies of your resume. Send an original, a good printed copy, or a photocopy.

What Happens to Your Resume?

Worth considering is what happens to your resume after it arrives in the office of a prospective employer. Your resume may go directly to the executive with the power to hire you, or it may pass through the more traditional channel of the personnel office. Professional personnel recruiters classify resumes that cross their desk in one of three ways:

1. **Target resume.** Forceful in presenting a summary of experience, qualifications, and education. Commands attention and leads to an invitation for a personal meeting.
2. **Ineffective resume.** Information jumbled, leaving no clear-cut

impression as to applicant's real potential. Applicant will be considered only if the employer is desperate to fill a position and has no other candidates on the horizon.

3. Dirty resume. Physical appearance of the document is sloppy and the manner in which background information is presented is messy. Such offerings are immediately consigned to the wastebasket.

Many firms do keep a file of applications for future needs. A man who applied for a sales manager's position he saw advertised in a newspaper submitted a well thought-out, concise, and effective resume. The company president, after consultation with his assistants, decided that the applicant was not exactly what they wanted for this particular opening, but the applicant was judged to be well suited for another division where the company needed individuals with good background, adaptability, and a sense of responsibility. The resume was kept on file and a courteous note was sent from a company vice-president informing the writer that he would be considered for a future opening.

Two months later, a position in industrial relations was created at the rank of vice-president. This same candidate was immediately called for an interview, and after an hour's conversation with the president and his assistants, he was offered the job. Today, he is president of the corporation.

His resume alone did not accomplish all this, but it was a fine first step. Executives realize that well-qualified employees are not easy to find. A resume can sell you properly and honestly if you have the potential.

Preparing to Interview

- Display a knowledge of the company and its products or services when you interview.
- Read as much company literature as possible before an interview.
- Acquire a general understanding of present-day business and industrial conditions. Study the job situation in your field to determine opportunities, working conditions, and wages offered.
- Have an idea of what you are seeking besides financial remuneration, e.g., medical plans, opportunity for advancement, pension program, or other benefits.
- Consult the appropriate business directory for possible interview leads.
- Assemble as many facts as possible about potential employers. Examine the companies employing persons of your skill and interest. Learn about the companies' products and the work that goes into them.

4

Model Resumes for Corporate and Management Executives

Most corporate and management executives are professionals who administer or help run businesses and other organizations. Some are managers who supervise, plan operations, and make company policy; others provide assistance to high-echelon officers. These include, for example, personnel directors who recruit and hire staff members, workers who handle employee problems, and persons who work in communications. The success or failure of an organization depends heavily on the leadership provided by management.

Nearly all administrative executive jobs require a college degree, although the specific area of study may vary. Some executives may be business administration or liberal arts graduates. Increasingly, persons have a background in a technical area such as engineering or science, and this will be an important trend in the 1980s.

Many officials use statistics and technical data in solving problems and making decisions. They rely heavily on up-to-date financial information and must be able to understand, prepare, and analyze financial reports. In addition, persons in this category must be tactful and be able to get along with colleagues and subordinates.

They may function in areas such as controlling, production, research and development, marketing and sales, programming and data processing, industrial relations and personnel, corporation law, and communications.

Problems confronting managers are many and varied: whether and how to manufacture a new model automobile, furnish a hotel lobby, advertise a store, supervise the production of a new chemical, create goodwill, guide financial investments, or manage real estate. Whatever the size of the organization, whether it employs a few people or many thousands, these executives contribute greatly to the success of the enterprise through their guidance and supervision.

Executives and other managerial personnel in business firms form the largest group of salaried officials. Several hundred thousand people in the executive category are connected with local, state, and federal government agencies and nonprofit organizations of many kinds. There are also a large number of other types of executives, such as purchasing agents and credit advisors, who are in specialized positions that are closely related to executive administrative work.

While these positions offer interesting, challenging, and rewarding work with relatively high earnings, they can be assumed only after extensive and specialized education and experience in the particular field. A broad knowledge of the field plus the ability to work well with others are prime prerequisites for this work.

The model resumes in this chapter are especially geared to corporate and management personnel.

FINANCE VICE-PRESIDENT

<u>Resume of</u>	Harry C. Fuller
	150 Prince Street
	Dallas, TX 75207 Telephone: (214) 697-8344

<u>Summary of</u> <u>Experience</u>

My personal characteristics and contributions to executive management are reflected in strong proven ability to
organize and supervise. I am familiar with the duties of a
controller-auditor, such as preparation of tax forms,
statutory and management reports, contract control,
client invoicing, credit and collection supervision. I am
able to take responsibility for all financial records and
report to the president or executive officer.

<u>Occupational</u> <u>Objective</u>

To utilize extensive management-administrative experience with a growing company where I can contribute to
the formulation of policies and help supervise general
management activities.

<u>Work</u> <u>Record</u>

Geophysical Research and Service Co.
Dallas, Texas

This is the world's leading oil and gas exploration
contractor, with ten corporations doing business in
twenty-two countries.

1972 to present

<u>Controller-Auditor</u>. Responsible for administration of
accounting for all corporations.

Responsibilities include: (1) preparation of tax, statutory, and statistical reports, domestic and foreign;
(2) cash working funds and corporate cash flow planning and
budget, including foreign exchange, restrictions, and
convertibility; (3) contract control, client invoicing,
credit and collection, export letters of credit and
collection, export letters of credit and documentation;
(4) asset records for ad valorem, franchise, use and sales
taxes, and insurance coverage; (5) payroll and disburse-
ment, personnel records of contract, deposits, savings,
and retirement, tax, and personal educations; and (6) cost
and budgetary accounting, field crews, area, and regional
offices. Maintain records for small oil field development.

Lambert Landscape Co.
Dallas, Texas

This company specializes in contract landscaping, real estate development, nursery products, architectural design consulting, interior decorating, retail specialties, and imported art objects and curios.

1968 to
1972

Chief Auditor. Employed to determine true financial status of the firm and development of operating controls. Responsibilities included the following: (1) programmed procedure to restore solvency and retain desired sources of supply, and arranged necessary financing; (2) negotiated and settled all past corporate and personal federal tax matters; (3) handled client credit extension, financing, and collection; (4) instituted cash and sales forecast and budgets; (5) devised and installed accounting system segregating departments and developed procedures, forms, reports; (6) established cost control and developed first standard costs in landscape contracting; and (7) devised bin and photographic inventory control system and equipment records.

G. H. Packwood Manufacturing Co.
St. Louis, Missouri

This company is a manufacturer of industrial skin cleansers.

1966 to
1968

Controller-Secretary Assistant to President. Responsible for all financial accounting records, credit and collection, payroll, wages, salaries and commissions, assets and insurance, local, state, and federal tax reports, corporate minutes and notices.

Due to improved methods, which led to economies and eliminated unnecessary expenditures, I was able to show a steady increase in profits during the two years of my employment with this company. By utilizing machinery in the operation of many jobs, I reduced labor costs.

Devised cost accounting methods for pricing and sales budgeting. Revised sales and commission contracts. Programmed and coordinated direct-mail promotion.

H & H Accounting Services
New York, New York

1964 to   This firm provides accounting services on a yearly basis
1966   for national and international companies.

                 Accountant. Part-time employment as accountant while
                 pursuing graduate studies.

Education   New York University, School of Business Administration,
                 New York, New York. B.S., June 1964. Special emphasis on
                 marketing, statistics, English composition, speech, psy-
                 chology; some specialized courses in marketing and eco-
                 nomics. Took part in intramural sports. Member of the Glee
                 Club. Expenses financed partially through scholarships,
                 summer jobs, and part-time employment during the college
                 year.

                 Columbia University School of Business, New York, New
                 York. M.S. in Business Administration, 1966. Took gradu-
                 ate courses in finance, management, and electronic data
                 processing procedures because of increasing use of compu-
                 ters in sales forecasting, distribution, cost analysis,
                 and other aspects of marketing research.

Professional   American Marketing Association
Affiliations   National Industrial Conference Board
                 Sales and Marketing Executives-International (SME-I)

Personal   Participate in local politics and community affairs.
Interests   Active during the last five years in the annual Red Cross
                 drive. Enjoy swimming and tennis in the summer. Widely
                 traveled in South America.

Personal   Married; three children: 5′ 9″; 160 pounds.
Data   Excellent health. Last physical: 1979.
                 Willing to relocate. Will travel.

Salary   In the range of $45,000.

References   Personal references available on request.

36 EFFECTIVE RESUMES FOR EXECUTIVES AND SPECIALIZED PERSONNEL

ACCOUNTANT

<u>Resume of</u>	Ruth T. Grier
	148 East Thirty-eighth Street
	New York, NY 10016 Telephone: (212) 688-7196

<u>Summary of</u>
<u>Experience</u>

Have eighteen years experience in the field of auditing and accounting. Accustomed to developing reports of different audits. Get along well with co-workers at all levels. Thoroughly familiar with programming and computing programs for financial and accounting control.

<u>Occupational</u>
<u>Objective</u>

To be associated with a firm that specializes in preparing budgets and cost studies, developing financial standards, and making reports after visiting and auditing different divisions or branches of the company.

<u>Work</u>
<u>Record</u>

<u>Heide & Son, Inc.</u>
New York, New York

1972 to
present

<u>Senior Auditor.</u> This is a prominent New York financial institution, where I have the opportunity to utilize my supervisory ability. My duties include training of auditors and accountant controllers for assignment at one of the branch offices. Among my other activities are

- evaluating internal controls,
- adapting auditing programs to test these controls,
- summarizing audit findings with the management of audited offices,
- preparing audit reports and evaluating assigned auditors.

About one-fourth of my time is spent in the field.

<u>Lifeline Cosmetics Co., Inc.</u>
New York, New York

1968 to
1972

This organization operates as a national and international manufacturer of cosmetics, with three domestic plants and six subsidiaries. It grosses approximately $200 million annually and employs 9,000 people.

<u>Senior Accountant.</u> Supervised a staff of approximately 350 people. Had full charge of general accounting, accounts payable, accounts receivable, payroll, billing and statistics, cost accounting, budgets, tax, and internal audit departments.

Model Resumes for Corporate and Management Executives   **37**

Completely reorganized the accounting department and put
it on a scientifically managed basis. Defined each job in
the department, outlined the duties and responsibilities,
and hired and trained the necessary supervisory personnel. Designed and revised forms and procedures and
completely mechanized the heavy-volume departments.

Devised and installed a system of international uniform
reports and charts, together with a supporting manual.
Established standard costs and operating budgets.

Assisted in the formulation of financial and financing
program, bank borrowings, and the floating of common stock
issues. Assisted in negotiations regarding the acquisition of three subsidiaries.

New York Financial Service, Inc
New York, New York

1965 to
1968

<u>Consolidation Accountant.</u> Assisted in the preparation of
consolidated financial statements and SEC filings, and
performed a variety of related functions. Member of the
financial management team of this multinational corporation with many divisions in continental United States, and
subsidiaries in several foreign countries.

In this position I exercised my oral and written communications abilities. Worked in special projects for the
corporate management. My financial studies and reports
helped the corporation's long- and short-range planning.

Peabody, Jones & Krugge, Inc.
New York, New York

1962 to
1965

This firm is one of the larger certified public accountant
organizations in the country. Started with them as a
junior accountant immediately after receiving my M.B.A.,
and successively became semisenior, senior, supervisor,
and manager.

<u>Managing Accountant.</u> Acted as the company's representa-
tive in contacts with top management of our clients.
Reported directly to the head of the firm. Handled all
types of assignments, including examination of financial
statements, review of clients' accounting systems, audits, and diverse tax work. Many assignments were in the
fields of chemicals, drugs, cosmetics, tanning, metal

fabricating, precision instruments, printing and publishing, oil, transporta tion, public utilities, banking,
and insurance.

Education

1960 to
1962

M.B.A. in Business Administration, June 1962, Hofstra
University, Hempstead, New York. General program of
studies with a view to obtaining broad accounting and
financial background. Second-year elective courses in
advanced accounting problems, financial management,
analysis of financial statements, legal aspects of business, current economic problems. Member of the Business
Club. Expenses financed by personal savings and a
fellowship.

1956 to
1960

B.S. in Commerce, June 1960, Hofstra University. Majored
in finance and economics, including industrial organization, business management, accounting , and personnel.
Member of the Chess Club. Expenses financed partially
through scholarship, summer jobs, and family funds.

**Professional
License**

Certified Public Accountant, New York State, 1962.

**Professional
Affiliation**

National Association of Cost Accountants (NAA), New York,
New York.

**Personal
Data**

Age 41. Married, one child. 5´4″, 120 pounds. Good
health. Willing to relocate. Will travel.

Salary

In the range of $30,000.

References

References on request.

BUDGET ANALYST

Robert H. Harrington
144 Wedgewood Drive
Evanston, IL 66021
Telephone: (312) 148-8450

Summary of
Experience

I possess a mainstream business orientation with demon-
strated competence in administration, finance, sales,
production, research, and development. My personal
characteristics and contributions are reflected in
strong proven abilities and aptitude for organization,
leader ship, and problem solving.

Occupational
Objective

To be connected with a corporation where I can use my
management abilities in order to contribute to the
administration and formulation of policies and to assist
in the general planning and development activities of the
organization.

As a budget manager, I hope to exercise my expertise in
finance operations control and to be instrumental in
strengthening a budget department.

Work
Record

Plant Builders, Inc.
Chicago, Illinois

1969 to
present

Budget Manager. Have worked for eleven years with this
corporation, which grosses over $300 million annually and
is still expanding. Extensive growth has created unusual
opportunity for enlarging my experience. My main duties
are concentrated in
- directing help in the development of engineering and
  construction programs,
- controlling the engineering and construction costs from
  project conception through completion,
- analyzing and forecasting variations in projected
  costs
- making recommendations to management for corrective
  action.

Hamilton Palmerly, Inc.
St. Louis, Missouri

1967 to
1969

Budget Director. While serving as budget director,
reporting directly to the executive vice-president, reorganized the financial administration, which increased
sales revenues 15 percent; upgraded merchandise quality;
increased inventory. Among my other achievements, I
- reduced cost of sales from 18 percent to 10 percent,
  converted sales policy from credit to cash basis, and

Page 1 of 2

                    initiated collection system netting 70 percent cash
                    from a/c to sixty days;
                    - streamlined budgeting, installed EDP accounting and
                    auditing, and cut administrative overhead 35 percent;
                    - converted cost-center service department to revenue-
                    producing division, decentralized operations to three
                    locations, and increased output over 200 percent in less
                    than two years.

Education   Northwestern University, Chicago, Illinois. B.S. in
                    Industrial Management, June 1965. Participated in under-
                    graduate course in industrial management designed for
                    students who combine aptitude for science and engineering
                    with administrative qualities. Emphasis on analysis of
                    business problems and managerial principles. Included use
                    of many rapidly developing mathematical and statistical
                    techniques for solving industrial problems. Senior the-
                    sis: "Programming in Business Management." Ranked in
                    upper sixth in graduating class of 450. Elected to Phi
                    Beta Kappa.

Military
Service   U.S. Navy, six months in South Pacific and remaining time
1965 to   in Germany.
1967

Early   Grew up in Highland Park, Illinois. Father was an execu-
Background   tive with a meat packing company. Attended Kent Prepara-
                    tory School, Seymour, Indiana. Member of Chess Club.
                    Graduated in top ten of class of eighty.

Outside   Campaigned for post of City Council representative last
Activities   year.
                    Organized community Man-of-the-Year award dinner.

Professional   American Accounting Society
Memberships   Data Processing Management Association, Park Ridge,
                    Illinois

Personal
Interests   Chess, sailing.

Personal   Born January 1944, Chicago, Illinois. Married, no children.
Data   Free to relocate.

Salary   In the range of $30,000.

References   Supplied on request.

Model Resumes for Corporate and Management Executives   **41**

PRODUCTION VICE-PRESIDENT

Resume of	Peter G. Stowell 680 Ramsey Street Fort Wayne, IN 62080 Telephone: (219) 786-2354

Summary of
Experience

Thirteen years of experience as plant and production manager. Consistently maintained delivery schedules in canning plant. Cut production costs in electronics factory. Developed satisfactory labor-management relations in both companies.

Occupational
Objective

To be associated with the manufacturing division of a corporation where my experience can be used to supervise work in such areas as process planning, methods engineering, plant layout, and automation.

Experience
Highlights

Global Electronics Co.
Fort Wayne, Indiana

1970 to
present

This company specializes in developing communications and avionic equipment, radar, radios, TV, and stereophonic high-fidelity sets. Employs more than 20,000 people. Annual average sales, $700 million.

Product Manager. This position requires expertise in cost accounting, experience as a process supervisor, knowledge of plant engineering and maintenance, and complete familiarity with labor laws and union contracts.

Oversee production activities of multiproduct manufacturing plant. Have established economical inventory levels for raw and finished goods. Introduced efficient methods that cut production costs 15 percent.

Great Falls Canning Co.
Paterson, New Jersey

1967 to
1970

Plant Manager. Directed all phases of production in ultramodern aluminum can manufacturing factory. Maintained the high standards for finished product and meeting delivery deadlines for which this company is noted. Met requirements of FDA. Scheduled night and day shifts to maximize efficient use of heavy machinery. Established cooperative relations between union members and management.

Page 1 of 2

Education   Stevens Institute of Technology, Union City, New Jersey.
                 Bachelor of Mechanical Engineering, 1967.
                 Graduated from Glen Rock High School, Glen Rock, New
                 Jersey, 1963.

Personal   Born: 5/16/45
Data   Married, two children
                 Excellent health

Salary   In the range of $30,000.

References   Available on request.

Resume of   Jeanette E. Clapp
                   49 Frenchtown Road
                   Bridgeport, CT 06606   Telephone: (203) 367-5476

Summary of   Fourteen years of experience as manufacturing engineer in
Experience   the field of communications equipment, aircraft engines,
                   and guided missiles. Supervised draftsmen. Worked with
                   outside vendors. Directed field activity for testing and
                   marketing new products.

Occupational   To attain a position with a U.S. firm in overseas
Objective   operations where I can utilize my experience as a manufac-
                   turing engineer and as a technical coordinator for new and
                   ongoing manufactured products.

Work   Merwin Tweedy Corp.
Record   Bridgeport, Connecticut

1974 to   Senior Product Engineer. Direct, monitor, and evaluate
present   tasks of three product engineers and five assistants
                   responsible for reliability of new products in the
                   business communications equipment field.

                   Responsible for the development and implementation of
                   service philosophy, procedures, and issuing of service
                   plans to be used by the field organization. Direct and
                   schedule the technical field support activity of new
                   products during the testing and marketing evaluation
                   stages.

                               Hamilton Standards, Inc.
                                Waterbury, Connecticut

1968 to   Manufacturing Process Engineer. Planned manufacturing
1974   processes, work station setups, and scheduling of activ-
                   ities in the manufacturing department for building and
                   assembling aircraft engines and accessories. Active in
                   liaison work with outside vendors on purchases of both
                   supplies and services.

                              Armstrong Engineering Inc.
                                Ann Arbor, Michigan

1966 to   Manufacturing Supervisor. Supervised fifty draftsmen.
1968   Outlined and scheduled manufacturing processes used in

Page 1 of 2

the assembling of cables, harnesses, and mechanical/elec-
trical assemblies for a guided missile program. Acted as a
customer's interface for all engineering modifications
resulting from product improvement and reliability
changes. Responsible for installation layouts and documentation of plant facilities used for testing and
evaluating aircraft engines and components under static
and dynamic conditions.

Education   Wayne State University, Detroit, Michigan. B.S. in Indus-
                   trial Engineering, 1966.

Personal   Enjoy tennis, skiing, and bicycling.
Interests

Relocation   Overseas assignment in Australia, Philippines, or New
Preference   Zealand.

Personal   Born: August 8, 1944
Data   Health: Excellent (Last
                     physical examination, 1979)
                   Marital Status: Single
                   Available: Immediately

Salary   Negotiable, in the range of $25,000.
Requirements

References   Upon request.

Model Resumes for Corporate and Management Executives **45**

Resume of   Nina Freudenberg
               693 Lexington Avenue
               New York, NY 10022   Telephone: (212) 534-7367

Summary of Experience

Twenty-four years experience in retail field. Started as assistant buyer for low-priced outlet specializing in manufacturers' discontinued items and publishers' remainders. Later became merchandising assistant for national chain of variety stores. Introduced computer controls for purchasing in present capacity with store that appeals to middle-income market.

Occupational Objective

To head buying department of a large chain store, department store, or national buying service.

Experience Highlights

Fraser's Department Store
New York, New York

1967 to present

Manager, Buying Department. Supervise purchasing of men's, women's, and children's wearing apparel; hardware; household goods; and drugs and cosmetics. Keep abreast of new items available on the market by attending trade shows and conventions and by constant reading of trade journals. Travel extensively searching for new merchandise. Visit factories and showings held throughout the country. Introduced computer system for maintaining inventories. Analyze past sales records to determine present price levels and customer preferences.

Marston Corporation
Brooklyn, New York

1960 to 1967

Merchandising Assistant. Interpreted demands and needs of variety store customers. Found and developed sources of merchandise that were attractive and priced to give a comfortable margin of profit to chain of stores in medium-sized cities. Met competition by originating promotions to increase sales of our merchandise.

Big Deal Outlet
Bronx, New York

1956 to 1960

Assistant Buyer. Joined the buying department of this store immediately after college. Talked with sales personnel to elicit their views and comments on merchandise

Page 1 of 2

the store was selling. Analyzed in detail items offered by
other stores, particularly goods advertised in newspapers.
Made summary reports of current trends for my immediate
superiors; these reports guided their purchasing.

Education   New York University, New York, New York. B.S. in Merchan-
                   dising, 1956. Major in merchandising, with courses in
                   marketing, buying, and retailing. Minors in English,
                   public relations, and accounting. Financed education by
                   working part time and through scholarships.

Professional   National Association of Purchasing Agents
Membership

Salary   Open to negotiation.

References   Available on request.

Model Resumes for Corporate and Management Executives **47**

Resume of   Stephen R. Longfellow
                1529 Cabrillo Avenue
                San Francisco, CA 94118   Telephone: (415) 679-4894

Summary of Experience

Traffic manager for past ten years for large company operating warehouses in mainland United States and Hawaii. Five years as technical adviser to freight traffic manager for food and chemical manufacturer. Instrumental in increasing annual revenues.

Occupational Objective

Position with an expanding firm that needs a traffic manager with extensive background in rail, truck, and water transportation.

Experience Highlights

American Consumer Industries, Inc.
San Francisco, California

This company owns and operates twenty-six refrigerated warehouses coast to coast and in Hawaii. Other activities include sale of ice for commercial use; sale and distribution of fuel oil; sale of electrical appliances, heating and air conditioning equipment, building materials, lumber, automobile supplies. Grosses more than $50 million yearly and employs approximately 10,000 people.

1970 to present

Traffic Manager. Made an exhaustive study of distribution charges in each of the company's sales areas and recommended relocation of several warehouses, which reduced freight charges approximately 20 percent in the South, and 15 percent west of Mississippi and east of the Rockies. My innovations resulted in a total dollar savings of approximately $500,000 a year.

Supervise traffic staff. Control expenditure of approximately $13 million a year in outbound and inbound freight charges.

Determine methods of shipment and routing of all freight from plants to warehouses and warehouses to consumers throughout the United States and Canada.

Supervise preparation of over seventy-five manuals showing how each product is to be routed to customer from the proper warehouse. Personally handle all inbound and outbound claims for shortage and damage. Established transit privileges, saving the company many thousands of dollars. Supervise the expediting and tracing of all inbound and outbound shipments.

Weatherall Company
Chicago, Illinois

1965 to
1970

This firm is a diversified food and chemical company.
Known for meats, soap, commercial fertilizers, and lawn
and garden plant foods. Domestically maintains fourteen
operating divisions, marketing products to all segments
of the U.S. economy.

Chief Rate Clerk. Technical adviser to freight traffic
manager. Instrumental in establishing a division standard for revenues which increased income by thousands of
dollars a year. Advised freight solicitors on settlement
of difficult claims.

Prepared proposals for changes in rates after first
establishing proper justification. Submitted these proposals to the Carriers Rate Committee. Responsible for
review and analysis of proposed rate changes, filing of
objections if required, and presentation of cases to the
committee. Expedited and traced freight cars, checked
rates, filed tariffs, and prepared statistical tonnage
reports. Responsible for quoting rates to the public and
handling diversions and reconsignments.

Education

Temple University, School of Business, Philadelphia,
Pennsylvania. B.S. in Business Administration, 1965.
Major in traffic and transportation, minor in mathematics. Included courses in economics of transportation,
industrial organization, and public policy and traffic.
Graduated cum laude. President of Delta Kappa Epsilon,
social fraternity. Member of the Economics Club.

Early
Background

Grew up in Laguna, California. Father was executive of an
insurance company. Prepared for college in Carson Long
Academy. Active in athletics.

Outside
Activities

Active in the Harbor Society of San Francisco. Participate
in student exchange program.

Professional
Memberships

National Transportation Association
Traffic Managers Club

Personal
Data

Born 7/2/44. Married, no children. Good health. Willing to
relocate or travel.

References

References available on request.

Model Resumes for Corporate and Management Executives **49**

RESEARCH AND DEVELOPMENT
EXECUTIVES

CORPORATE PLANNING AND DEVELOPMENT VICE-PRESIDENT

Resume of

Jack B. Henderson
107 Sherwood Drive
Englewood, NJ 07632   Telephone: (201) 713-9897

Summary of
Experience

Fourteen years experience in market research: three years
working on sales analysis and new product studies for
rubber company; four years as supervisor of research
department in advertising agency; past seven years as
director of research department of refrigeration equipment manufacturer.

Occupational
Objective

To become a corporate planning and development executive
with either an industrial firm or an advertising agency
which requires a broad background of survey and analysis,
report preparation and personal contact, as well as proven
administrative ability.

Experience
Highlights

Franklin Refrigeration Co.
Fairlawn, New Jersey

This is one of the largest manufacturers of air conditioning and refrigeration equipment for household and industrial uses in the country.

1973 to
present

Director of Research Department. Supervise activities of
market research department. Projects are aimed at promoting efficacy of various divisions of the company.

Supervise preparation and analysis of studies of marketing problems, sales and profit forecasts, competition,
product improvement, pricing policies, distribution
methods, sales, and sales promotion and advertising
plans. Prepare reports for top management.

Advance Advertising Agency, Inc.
New York, New York

This agency handles consumer products. Maintains offices
in New York, Chicago, and Los Angeles.

1969 to
1973

Supervisor of Research Department. Worked closely with
clients in the electrical appliance field, devising and
conducting market surveys, analyzing and reporting market
trends, and developing consumer-reaction reports.

Page 1 of 2

Yale Rubber & Tire Co.
Akron, Ohio

This company is a leading tire manufacturer with extensive
international operations; it also manufactures various
consumer products.

1966 to   Assistant to Research Director. Participated in projects
1969   involving internal and external analysis. Aided in formu-
           lating plans and conducting programs to determine consu-
           mer reactions to products, policies, and advertising.

           Worked on sales analysis and forecast studies; ware-
           housing and new product studies; analysis of advertising
           effectiveness and numerous problems relating to the
           manufacturing activities of the company; and analysis of
           wholesale and retail operations.

Education New York University, School of Business Administration,
           New York, New York. B.S. in Economics, June 1964. Courses
           in marketing, economics, statistics, English composi-
           tion, speech, psychology. Tuition financed through
           scholarships, summer jobs, and part-time employment
           during the college year.

           Columbia University, New York, New York. M.B.A., 1966.
           Took graduate courses in electronic data-processing
           procedures to use in sales forecasting, distribution,
           cost analysis, and other aspects of marketing research.

Early   Grew up in Great Neck, Long Island. Father was a depart-
Background ment store executive. Worked for Nassau County Parks
           Department during summer vacations.

Professional   American Marketing Association
Affiliations   National Industrial Conference Board
               Sales and Marketing Executives Association

Personal   Willing to relocate, will travel.
Data

Salary   Negotiable, in the $30,000 range.

References Available on request.

Model Resumes for Corporate and Management Executives **51**

PLANNING AND DEVELOPMENT MANAGER

Grant S. Jourdan
700 Clarendon Avenue
St. Louis, MO 63108
Telephone: (314) 425-7981

Summary of Experience

Fifteen years experience in the field of development and planning for manufacturing companies. Originated strategy for soap company which succeeded in outstripping competition. Opened up new opportunities for revenue through mergers and acquisitions.

Occupational Objective

To be a key individual on the management team, assisting in the development and execution of plans for business growth in a firm that specializes in the technology required for all phases of information collection and processing systems.

Experience

Blake & Rogers, Inc.
St. Louis, Missouri

1974 to present

Development and Planning Manager. This is a major manufacturer of roller and thrust bearings transmission units. Developed new business from company headquarters through diversification, mergers, and acquisitions. This position carries responsibility for the planning of marketing and sales objectives for short- and long-term growth as well as for directing marketing activities to insure attainment of goals. I have responsibility for planning new business to achieve optimum marketing of products.

Merwin & Thomas, Inc.
Indianapolis, Indiana

1969 to 1974

Manager of New Business Development. This is a leading manufacturer of tags and labels. Because of my technical training and experience I was able to find and engage technical assistants to develop new products and technology.

Reported directly to the president and supervised twenty-five individuals in my department. I directed the development of new products for paper, fabric, and foil tags and labels, and new imprinting technology. Played a key role in product development and product distribution.

Page 1 of 2

52 EFFECTIVE RESUMES FOR EXECUTIVES AND SPECIALIZED PERSONNEL

McKinley, Cravens & Florin, Inc.
Dallas, Texas

1965 to 1969	Development Associate. Member of the commercial planning division staff of this firm, which manufactures floor waxes, finishes, soaps, disinfectants, and insecticides. Specialized in market identification, technical and commercial planning, and strategy formulation and implementation.
Educational Background	Abilene Christian College, Abilene, Texas. B.S. in Industrial Engineering. Graduated magna cum laude, May 1963, in class of over 400 graduates. Member of Alpha Chi (honorary scholastic fraternity). Financed college expenses working part time with a firm of consulting engineers.
Military Service	Served in U.S. Air Force, 1963-65. Honorably discharged as staff sergeant.
Professional/ Specialists Memberships	Systems and Procedures Association American Society of Industrial Engineers
References	Available on request.

PRODUCT DEVELOPMENT MANAGER

Louis B. Cohen
450 River Road
Lambertville, NJ 08530
Telephone: (609) 611-5789

Summary of Experience	Eighteen years inaugurating and supervising planning systems for chemical and electronics companies. Improved efficiency of operations and contributed to steady increase of profits.
Occupational Objective	Managerial position in technical program utilizing my background in systems acquisition, systems management, configuration, and data management.

Experience
Highlights

National Chemical and Food Corp.
Trenton, New Jersey

1971 to
present

Director of Technical Planning. Established and maintain technical research planning system. Direct development and use of appropriate analyses and reports. Insure that technical researchers and business colleagues utilize the system for maximum production. Recommend improvements in the design and operation of the system.

Lea and Holt Chemical Corp.
Philadelphia, Pennsylvania

1967 to
1971

Production Supervisor. Developed and implemented configuration management plan. System encompassed radars, computers, and navigation subsystems. Reviewed and approved all engineering changes and controlled implementation of changes.

Contributed to the test and integration plan for twenty types of equipment through the development of a laboratory facility.

Gonzalez Electronics Corp
Pittsburgh, Pennsylvania

1962 to
1967

Assistant Supervisor. Participated in conducting SONAR FPS 35 radar and small-boat radar programs. Developed control procedures and critiques of operating organizations. Devised detailed production plans and schedules.

Page 1 of 2

Education   Princeton University, Princeton, New Jersey. B.S. in
                     Engineering, with honors, June 1962. Majored in mechani-
                     cal engineering. Electives: English, history, biochemis-
                     try. Senior thesis: "Functional Design for Modern
                     Industry." Ranked in upper tenth of graduating class of
                     380. Elected to Phi Beta Kappa. Member of varsity football
                     team, three years; captain, senior year. College tuition
                     financed with partial scholarship and family funds.

Early   Grew up in Haddonfield, New Jersey. Father was a chemist
Background   for Northeastern Refining Company. Attended Oxford
                     Academy, Pleasantville, N.J. Third in class of 100.
                     Elected president of class in senior year.

Memberships   Princeton Club
                     Rotary International
                     American Society of Mechanical Engineers

Personal   Married, no children.
Data   Good health.
                     Willing to relocate.

References   Available on request.
and Portfolio

Model Resumes for Corporate and Management Executives   **55**

ADVERTISING VICE-PRESIDENT

Resume of	Harold M. Alberts
	120 Columbus Avenue
	Glendale, CA 91203 Telephone: (213) 482-6985

Summary of Experience

Twenty-three years experience in the field of advertising:
- Served as account executive, advertising manager, copywriter, and media director.
- Developed campaigns for new products and expanded marketing possibilities.
- Conducted and supervised marketing analyses for future campaigns of clients.
- Supervised preparation of promotion brochures and booklets.
- Prepared copy for predetermined audience and media.
- Selected print and broadcast media for yearly budgets.

Occupational Objective

To be associated with an advertising agency, in an executive capacity, or the advertising department of a multinational firm.

Work Record

Luria, Clark Corp.
Los Angeles, California

Advertising agency with ten offices in the United States and overseas; staff of more than 1,000 employees.

1968 to present

Account Executive. Handle several of this agency's most important accounts. Among my responsibilities is maintenance of good relations with clients.

Study clients' sales and advertising problems, develop new plans to meet their needs, and secure clients' approval of proposed programs.

In bringing new ideas to every level of the agency's projects, both theoretical and practical aspects of my advertising training and background are continually used.

Page 1 of 3

United Chemical Co.
Detroit, Michigan

Manufacturer of chemicals, pharmaceuticals, plastics and
resins, synthetic fibers, and personal care products.
Company has ten plants and laboratories in the United
States and five in foreign capitals. Employs 10,000 men
and women.

1961 to 1968	**Advertising Manager.** Selected appropriate media for products and prepared the advertising budget. Directed agencies handling our accounts. Established policy and strategy for reaching target audience. Set guidelines for the advertising agency in planning promotional programs. Supervised execution of the plans, including presentation of technical studies, display cards, and other promotional material.

Fraser Advertising Co.
Cleveland, Ohio

Advertising agency with four branches in the United
States.

1959 to 1961	**Advertising Copywriter.** Created copy, slogans, and text to attract buyers and new customers. Collected information about the products and conducted research for appropriate markets.

Ogden Dougal Tractor Co.
San Francisco, California

Manufacturers of tractors and equipment sold worldwide.

1957 to 1959	**Assistant Media Director.** Assisted in selection of the most effective media for reaching the maximum number of prospective buyers at the least cost. Compiled data on advertising costs in all media, comparing the relative size and composition of the audience reached in various parts of the country by specialized publications, broadcasting stations, television programs, and other media.

Model Resumes for Corporate and Management Executives   **57**

<u>Education</u>	Master of Science, Syracuse University, New York 1957 Graduate courses in advertising and copywriting Bachelor of Arts, University of California at Berkeley, 1953
<u>Professional</u> <u>Affiliations</u>	Advertising Federation of America (AFA), Los Angeles International Advertising Association, San Francisco
<u>Personal</u> <u>Recognition</u>	President of Glendale Rotary Club Award from Community Service Council for service to youth.
<u>Military</u> <u>Service</u>	U.S. Navy. Upon graduation from college, entered Officer Candidate School. Released from active duty, June 1955.
<u>Personal</u> <u>Data</u>	Born 6/28/31 Married, two children Health excellent
<u>References</u>	Furnished on request.

58 EFFECTIVE RESUMES FOR EXECUTIVES AND SPECIALIZED PERSONNEL

MARKETING AND SALES VICE-PRESIDENT

Janet L. O'Neal
130 East Thirty-ninth Street
New York, NY 10016
Telephone: (212) 755-2350

Summary of Experience

Twenty-one years with pharmaceutical company, during which I moved from assistant in the customer service department to sales manager. Contributed to expansion of company and increased profits, with sales volume rising steadily by 20 percent during past five years.

Objective

Position as marketing and sales vice-president where my experience and training can be fully utilized and where there is an opportunity for further advancement and increased responsibility.

Experience Highlights

American Pharmaceutical Corp.
New York, New York

This organization, with corporate headquarters in New York, maintains laboratories and factories in New Jersey and employs approximately 6,400 scientists, administrators, clerical, and semiskilled workers. Grosses more than $750 million annually. Since inception, it has developed formulas for 210 dispensing specialties, including tablets, liquids, ointments and injectibles.

1970 to present

Sales Manager. Organized marketing operations and hired and trained sales staff. Composed label copy and literature, revising it periodically to conform with changing government regulations. Established and edited catalog listing pharmaceutical specialties. Work with controller in determining price list. Assign sales territories and devise incentive plans.

1959 to 1970

Began in customer service department on graduating from college. Helped revise and improve shipping department.

Promoted to purchasing department in 1962. Was responsible for the preparation and submission of all formal quotations to municipal and state institutions and industrial buyers.

Page 1 of 2

Assistant Manager. Became assistant manager in 1965. Handled major portion of sales correspondence. Methods introduced contributed to annual rise of 20 percent in sales volume.

Education   New York University, B.S. in Marketing, 1959

Memberships   American Trade Association
                   Board of Directors, YMCA of Greater New York
                   American Marketing Asociation

Personal   Married, one child
Data   Willing to relocate or travel

References   Available on request.

60   EFFECTIVE RESUMES FOR EXECUTIVES AND SPECIALIZED PERSONNEL

Resume of   John W. Meyers
             149 Martin Luther King Boulevard
             Roxbury, MA 02119   Telephone (617) 428-7295

Experience   Have developed contacts with purchasing agents and buyers
             of large companies throughout the country during the past
             seventeen years. Have supervised sales force in field of
             consumer products; also devised strategies for campaigns
             for power tools and industrial machinery.

Occupational To direct sales program for manufacturer of electrical
Objective   appliances for home use or heavy equipment for industry.
             Seek company in need of an aggressive sales manager to
             improve sales performance, a firm that is willing to
             embark on original and innovative programs to open new
             territories for product sales.

Work   Home Appliance Mfg. Co.
Experience   Boston, Massachusetts

1970 to   Sales Executive/Assistant to the President. In charge of
present   handling two hard-goods lines of consumer products for
             this fast-growing enterprise. Supervise the sales manage-
             ment team, assist the president in execution of sales
             strategies, identify new sales opportunities, and main-
             tain an open line of communication with the company's
             sales force. My position requires creative sales and
             marketing ability. I travel about 30 percent of the time.

                         Chemical Air Pollution Control Co.
                                Houston, Texas

1966 to   Technical Sales Manager. This firm provides pollution
1970   abatement services to the electric power, iron and steel,
             and coal and ferroalloy industries. It is acknowledged as
             one of the leaders in the field and has expanded rapidly in
             the last decade to meet the critical needs of industry. I
             organized and directed the sales efforts of company
             representatives.

Page 1 of 2

Model Resumes for Corporate and Management Executives **61**

Electric Tools Manufacturing Co.
Chicago, Illinois

1963 to   Assistant Sales Manager. This firm is a well-established
1966   company with a strong leadership position in portable
               electric appliances and tools. My position required a
               thorough knowledge of sales promotion and marketing
               techniques to sell products through major retail
               outlets. I helped to initiate and administer sales plans
               that achieved targeted results through direction and
               motivation of the national sales force.

Education   Tufts University, Medford, Massachusetts. B.S. in Busi-
               ness Administration, 1963. Special emphasis on marketing,
               statistics, English, speech, and psychology. Took part in
               intramural sports. President of Delta Kappa Epsilon
               fraternity. Member of the Glee Club. Expenses covered
               partially through scholarships, summer jobs, and part-
               time employment during the college year.

Professional   American Marketing Association
Affiliations   National Industrial Conference Board
               Sales and Marketing Executives-International

Personal   Participate in local politics and community affairs.
Interests   Active during the last five years in the annual Red Cross
               drive.

Personal   Born 8/15/41. Married, three children.
Data   Willing to relocate.

References   Available on request.

62   EFFECTIVE RESUMES FOR EXECUTIVES AND SPECIALIZED PERSONNEL

Resume of   Jane R. Hilton
                800 Brooks Avenue
                Caldwell, NJ 07006   Telephone: (201) 396-9573

Experience

More than tenty years of experience in marketing research. Strong background in sales and market analysis, sales forecasting, market potential studies, and performance appraisal reporting.

Objective

To fill position of marketing research manager with a firm where I will have the opportunity to introduce innovative techniques, such as consideration of how biorhythms in human beings affect research results.

Occupational Experience

Blake Pharmaceutical Manufacturing Company, Inc.
Bloomfield, New Jersey

1970 to present

Market Research Analyst. This firm specializes in proprietary drugs and toiletry production. I have a variety of responsibilities and report directly to the Marketing executive vice-president. Act as liaison between marketing management and advertising agencies. Explore possibilities of introducing new products to public. Travel extensively to feel pulse of consumers. Conduct research from questionnaire to final report.

Marketing Research Associates
Rochester, New York

1965 to 1970

Marketing Manager. Researched market conditions on local, regional, and national level to determine the sales potential of client's product or service.

Planned forms used to obtain necessary information for analysis. Examined statistical data on sales and wholesale/retail trade trends to forecast future sales projections.

Eastern Marketing Research Corp.
Greenwich, Connecticut

1958 to 1965

Marketing Research Assistant. In charge of gathering information about our competitors, as well as analyzing their prices and methods of operation.

Page 1 of 2

Collected data on buying habits and preferences of prospective customers.

Education   B.S. in Business Administration, 1956, Hofstra University, Hempstead, New York. Majored in marketing. Other subjects taken in college were economics, industrial organization, business management, personnel. Member of the Philatelic Club and Glee Club. Expenses financed partially through scholarship, summer jobs, and family funds.

                   M.B.A. in Marketing, 1958, New York University, New York, New York. General program of studies with a view toward obtaining broad marketing research background. Master's thesis: "Importance of Distribution of Consumer Products."

Affiliations   American Marketing Association
                   American Industrial Development Council, Incorporated

Salary   In the mid-twenties, plus fringe benefits.

References   On request.

64   EFFECTIVE RESUMES FOR EXECUTIVES AND SPECIALIZED PERSONNEL

PROGRAMMERS AND COMPUTER
PERSONNEL

PROGRAMMER

Resume of
James E. Collier
1029 Bendon Road
Baltimore, MD 21208   Telephone: (301) 679-2136

Summary of
Experience
Twenty-four years of engineering, programming, and program management experience with BSSE, MBA, PE. Thorough knowledge of minicomputer systems that use unique peripherals. Worked in the fields of ophthalmics and publishing.

Occupational
Objective
To join a corporation where advanced experience in different phases of systems programming is needed.

Employment
History

Ophthalmic Products Corp.
Baltimore, Maryland

1969 to
present
Systems Programmer. This company is one of the leaders in the field of ophthalmic products, scientific instruments, and consumer products. Use DOS/VS, OS/VS, and CICS in programming. Obtained complete knowledge of programming language and techniques in present capacity.

Programmed Engineering Corp.
Needham, Massachusetts

1963 to
1969
Programmer-Engineer. Developed new systems of real-time minicomputer-based software for the training of operational and maintenance personnel associated with large-scale DOD Command and Control Systems. Participated in the evolution of the system from the initial conceptual definition and design through integration, checkout, and installation.

Communications Industries, Inc.
Somerset, New Jersey

1956 to
1963

Assistant Programmer. Company is book publisher. Installation operated with an IBM 370 running under release of
DOS/VS power, communications with local CRTs by means of
DUCs. Other software included Easytrieve, Librarian,
CA-Sort, and TFAST. Minicomputer linked several branch
facilities via telecommunications. Supervised systems
and software maintenance, evaluated and installed new
hardware and software, and provided technical education
and assistance to users.

Education

Illinois Institute of Technology, Chicago, Illinois,
1952-1956, B.S. in Industrial Engineering. Majored in
industrial engineering, studying basic engineering,
basic science and mathematics, engineering science, and
design. Other studies included humanities, social sciences, and management subjects. Obtained exceptional
marks in production planning and control, cost analysis,
operations research, and industrial relations. Financed
education through G.I. Bill and parttime work.

Military
Service

U.S. Army. 1950-1952. Attended Officer Candidate School
for eight months. Completed seven-week Finance Officer
Orientation Course and ten-week Finance Basic Course at
the Army Finance School, Fort Benjamin Harrison, Indiana.
Assigned to Headquarters, Fifth U.S. Army, Chicago,
Illinois.

Affiliations

Association for Computing Machinery
Data Processing Management Association
American Federation of Information Processing Societies
Board of Directors, YMCA
Society of Friends of the Industrial Museum

Personal
Data

Born 1932. Married, one son.
Willing to relocate.
Willing to travel.

References

On request.

Resume of   Mary R. Wilson
                435 East Sixty-ninth Street
                New York, NY 10021   Telephone: (212) 657-7879

Experience   Eleven years of experience working with computer equip-
                ment and supervising personnel. Prepared programs for
                physicians and engineers engaged in research. Analyzed
                economic and statistical data. Devised programs to obtain
                necessary information.

Objective   To be connected with a private firm or government depart-
                ment where the background of a well-trained scientific
                data processor can be used in the research and development
                of future projects.

Employment   American Data Processing Service, Inc.
                              New York, New York

1973 to   Scientific Data Processing Supervisor. Work with physi-
present   cians and engineers, helping in research and analysis of
                different problems. Devised programs to obtain the essen-
                tial information.

                         All-Over Data Information
                           Jersey City, New Jersey

1969 to   Data Processing Technician. Assisted in developing pro-
1973   grams for union reports, payrolls, brokerage houses, and
                insurance companies. General assistant for major instal-
                lation; supervised all types of equipment and computers.

Education   A.A., New York Institute of Technology, New York, New
                York, 1969. Graduated George Washington High School, New
                York, New York, 1967.

Membership   Data Processing Management Association

Personal   Born 1949
Data   Good health
                Married
                Will relocate

Salary   Open to negotiation.

References   Available on request.

19--

<u>Resume of</u>	John L. Glanvelle 500 Montgomery Avenue West Philadelphia, PA 19122 Telephone (215) 622-6070

<u>Summary of
Experience</u>

Diversified background in business operations and systems applications. Experienced in the maintenance of process computer systems, including hardware and software analysis. Have developed techniques for training assistants.

<u>Occupational
Objective</u>

A position as electronic data processing analyst with a company where my experience and managerial skills can be used to full advantage; a position with challenge and growth potential.

<u>Work
Record</u>

<u>Software Design and Testing Corp.</u>
Belleville, Pennsylvania

1970 to
present

<u>Programmer Analyst</u>. Attached to the computer center of the corporation. Guide the development and implementation of diverse management-information systems. Take active part in programming and design of small-to-medium-size systems. Carry the project from beginning through completion.

<u>Interstate Electric Appliance Co.</u>
San Francisco, California

1965 to
1970

<u>Marketing Development Program Supervisor</u>. Developed an accounts-receivable computer application that was highly approved by top management. Tasks included flowcharting, programming, and documenting. Did demonstrations for our sales staff.

<u>Global Oil Company</u>
New York, New York

1961 to
1965

<u>Price and Billing Supervisor</u>. Prepared invoices to international and domestic affiliates, the United States government, and domestic customers for crude and refined oil products. Originated all allowances, credits, and commissions applicable to the invoices. Assisted in various details involved in the preparation of the company profit-and-loss statement.

Page 1 of 2

Education   B.S. in Business Administration, 1959, Drexel Institute
                   of Technology, Philadelphia, Pennsylvania.
                   M.B.A. in Industrial Management, 1961, Temple University,
                   Philadelphia, Pennsylvania. IBM courses in advanced sys-
                   tems design, 1401/1410 programming, S/360, operating sys-
                   tems, and COBOL.

Professional   Membership Chairman, Data Processing Management Associa-
Association   tion, Main Line Chapter.

Personal   Born 1937. Married, four children.
Data

References   Will be furnished on request.

Resume of	Alex J. Harding 100 Twenty-ninth Avenue Vancouver, WA 98663 Telephone: (206) 825-9765

Summary of
Experience

Fourteen years in data processing, working with punchers, tabulators, calculators, interpreters, reproducers, and collators. Systems which I introduced increased efficiency in operation of accounting and sales departments.

Objective

To supervise data processing department of large corporation that requires an expert who is familiar with the latest machinery and techniques in this rapidly changing field.

Work
Record

A & R Copying Corporation
Vancouver, Washington

1970 to
present

Data Systems Supervisor. Replaced obsolete machines; eliminated three verifiers; and reduced the work force operating punchers, tabulators, calculators, interpreters, reproducers, sorters, and collators. Retrained personnel. Changes have resulted in greater productivity at lower cost.

Medallion Company of America
Rochester, New York

1966 to
1970

Assistant Director, Programming Division. Assisted in developing plans and procedures for effective use of data processing machines. Tested equipment and assisted in supervising programming designed to automate routine office and clerical functions.

Used the IBM 1401 for running tapes for large-scale computer systems and stored data programs.

Education

Massachusetts Institute of Technology, Cambridge, Massachusetts. B.S. in Industrial Management, 1966. Undergraduate course in industrial management designed for students who combine aptitude for science and engineering with administrative abilities. Included use of many rapidly developing mathematical and statistical techniques for solving industrial problems. Senior thesis: "Programming in Business Management."

Professional   Data Processing Management Association
Memberships   Association for Computing Machinery

Outside   Interested in politics; member of local political club.
Activities   Active in community charity organizations.

Personal   Born 1944, Worcester, Massachusetts. Married, no chil-
Data   dren. Wife is registered nurse. Free to relocate.

Salary   In the $25,000 range. Salary history on request.

References   Available on request.

INDUSTRIAL RELATIONS AND
PERSONNEL EXECUTIVES

Resume of   Pamela O. Foster
                 450 Drury Lane
                 St. Louis, MO 63122   Telephone (314) 512-7941

Summary of   Sixteen years of experience in testing and evaluating
Experience   personnel. Successful negotiations of union contracts
                 have resulted in no strikes during my present tenure.

Occupational   To be associated with a company as industrial relations
Objective   and personnel manager where full use can be made of my
                 diversified experience in the field.

Employment   Automotive Parts Mfg. Co.
Record   St. Louis, Missouri

                 This firm manufactures automotive accessories and compo-
                 nent parts. Does an annual volume of approximately $250
                 million; operates three plants; and employs about 3,500
                 people.

1971 to   Industrial Relations Vice-President. Formulate company
present   policies. Direct a comprehensive personnel and industrial
                 relations program for the whole company. Handle all labor
                 relations, including contract negotiations for four
                 international unions.

                 Devised, prepared, and installed a supervisory and
                 employee training program which was accepted and approved
                 by the union. Developed and installed a formal wage
                 program which eliminated many inequities previously
                 existing. Handle all health, accident, and life insurance
                 and workmen's compensation, pensions, and other benefits.

                 Have installed a safety-and-fire-prevention program and
                 conducted regular classes in the various plants. Have
                 lowered the accident rate to less than 1 percent from 2.2
                 percent.

                 Installed testing for better selection of both hourly and
                 salaried personnel. Complete maintenance of all employee
                 records. Simplified employee records system, thereby
                 eliminating unnecessary duplication of information.

Page 1 of 3

Aerospace Instruments, Inc.
Des Moines, Iowa

This firm manufactures precision instruments for the aeronautical field. It employs approximately 20,000 people and grosses $180 million yearly.

1968 to
1971

Manager of Industrial Relations. Supervised and coordinated a comprehensive personnel and labor relations program.

Participated in negotiations for two union contracts and supervised their administration.

Responsible for employment, training, safety, wage and salary administration, and employee welfare.

ARC Radio Mfg. Co., Inc.
Louisville, Kentucky

This firm manufactures industrial radios for commercial and military use, operates two plants, and employs approximately 6,500 people.

1964 to
1968

Employment Manager. Fully responsible for setting up a program for hiring all classes of skilled and nonskilled personnel.

Supervised a staff of twelve interviewers and seven clerical personnel.

Maintained full records of employment, training, and safety. Installed a screening and testing program to better select trades and crafts people. Supervised the keeping of all statistical records, personnel records, and draft deferments.

Made weekly reports to management on the employment situation in the plant, area, and state, as it applied to the industry.

Education

B.S. in Industrial Relations and Personnel, 1964. Oklahoma State University, Stillwater, Oklahoma. Majored in industrial relations. Courses included development of labor organizations; personnel management; labor-management relations; collective bargaining; human relations; and accounting.

Professional Affiliations	American Society for Personnel Administration Industrial Relations Research Association
Personal Interests	Have traveled extensively in Europe and Latin America. Take active part in the annual March of Dimes campaign. Born 8/3/42.
References	Available on request.

74 EFFECTIVE RESUMES FOR EXECUTIVES AND SPECIALIZED PERSONNEL

<u>Resume of</u>	Raymond L. Fisher 1010 North Dearborn Street Chicago, IL 60610 Telephone: (312) 455-0525

<u>Summary of</u>
<u>Experience</u>

Thirteen years of experience in personnel and labor relations work. Familiar with electrical scoring machines and computer devices adapted to personnel field. Have participated in arbitration proceedings and collective bargaining negotiations.

<u>Objective</u>

To head the personnel or industrial relations department of a multinational firm where my ability to interview, supervise, classify, and counsel employees, and negotiate union contracts will contribute to smooth operations of company and to increased efficiency and profits.

<u>Experience</u>
<u>Record</u>

<u>National Hardware Mfg. Corp.</u>
Skokie, Illinois

1971 to
present

<u>Labor Relations Manager</u>. Prepare preliminary reports for company representation at grievance hearings; participate in arbitration proceedings and collective bargaining negotiations; and work closely with union leaders to maintain uninterrupted production. Developed employee communications and incentive programs. Regularly review work performance to determine salary increases.

<u>Aluminum Mfg. Corp.</u>
Evanston, Illinois

1967 to
1971

<u>Assistant Personnel Manager</u>. Assisted in auditing personnel records and collecting data on human resources. Used electrical scoring machines and computing devices to appraise applicants and employees being considered for promotion. Handled benefits and service records and conducted employee interviews. Participated in the design and development of multiplant industrial relations activity.

<u>Education</u>

Temple University, School of Business Administration, Philadelphia, Pennsylvania. B.S. in Business Administration, 1967. Courses included economics, industrial organization, public policy, and psychology.

Page 1 of 2

Professional   Delta Nu Alpha, national personnel fraternity
Memberships   Personnel Managers Club of Chicago

Outside   Member of the Chicago Athletic Club and North Shore Bridge
Activities   Club. Enjoy fishing, swimming, and tennis during summer.

Personal   Born 2/26/45. Single. Good health.
Data   Willing to relocate or travel.

Salary and   Salary open to negotiation. References available on
References   request.

76   EFFECTIVE RESUMES FOR EXECUTIVES AND SPECIALIZED PERSONNEL

Resume of   Ruth H. Furman
                4 Barksdale Road
                Richmond, VA 23221   Telephone: (804) 921-8679

Summary of   Have extensive experience in labor relations, union
Experience   contract negotiations, EEO policies, and recruitment of
                top-level executives gained through employment with large
                manufacturing companies.

Objective   To be connected with a large corporation where my exten-
                sive professional background in personnel and industrial
                relations can be utilized for mutual benefit.

Employment   Whittaker Chemical Co.
                    Richmond, Virginia

1970 to   Personnel Director for large chemical company with
present   branches througout the South and total sales of $300
                million annually. Have reached top level in my area of
                expertise. Responsibilities include establishing poli-
                cies and procedures regarding

                — union contract administration,
                — employee benefits administration,
                — wage and salary administration,
                — EEO and affirmative action plan.

               Longacre Industries, Inc.
                    Atlanta, Georgia

1964 to   Employment Manager for one of the world's leading computer
1970   manufacturers, which maintains branches in ten states.
                Full responsibility for recruitment and placement of
                manufacturing professionals. Utilized such sources as
                display and classified advertising in newspapers and
                technical journals, employment agencies, executive
                searchers, and personal contacts.

               Claremont Crane Co.
                    Louisville, Kentucky

1960 to   Field Employee Relations Representative with this com-
1964   pany, which manufactures hoists, overhead cranes, and
                monorail systems. Visited company plants in Georgia,

Page 1 of 2

Tennessee, Indiana, and Arkansas. Assisted in administer-
ing EEO policies and union contract negotiations. Position required extensive travel, which was one of my
reasons for leaving.

Education   Temple University School of Commerce, Philadelphia, Penn-
                 sylvania. M.B.A. in Industrial Relations, 1960.
                 Drexel Institute of Technology, Philadelphia, Pennsylva-
                 nia. B.S. in Business Administration, 1958.

Memberships   Data Processing Management Association
                 Employment Management Association
                 Personnel and Industrial Relations Association

Personal   Born 4/20/37.
Data   Health excellent.
                 Single.

Salary   Open to negotiation, in $35,000-$40,000 range.

References   Will be furnished on request.

Resume of	Clarence C. Isaza
	98 Longmeadow Avenue
	Worcester, MA 01606 Telephone: (617) 594-5948

Summary of Experience

Twenty-two years of experience in planning, developing, and evaluating industrial training programs. Worked closely with managers and potential managers at all levels.

Occupational Objective

To serve as training/retraining director for a company that needs development of innovative policies for introducing modern techniques and procedures to personnel in all classifications.

Experience Highlights

American Electronic Equipment Corp.
Boston, Massachusetts

1969 to present

Training Program Director. Developed reference tests, did media selection, and evaluated instruction for rapidly expanding company in need of an intensive training/retraining program. Applied systems approach to the design of instruction. Company is moving to Arizona, but I prefer to remain in the Northeast.

World Wide Insurance Co.
Hartford, Connecticut

1963 to 1969

Training and Development Manager. Prepared and conducted in-house training programs. Evaluated external programs in cooperation with outside training organizations. Focused on developing effective analytical report-writing skills. Conducted orientation programs and collected data to be used in all training courses.

Automatic Engineering Co.
Chicago, Illinois

1958 to 1963

Assistant Training Manager. Participated in all phases of training: analysis, program development, instruction, and postinstruction evaluation. The program put special emphasis on first-line supervisory and management training of sales and marketing personnel.

Education   University of Chicago, Chicago, Illinois. M.A. in Person-
                   nel Psychology, 1958. Among courses taken were psychology
                   of adjustment, modern training and retraining techniques
                   and their application, and personnel management. Thesis:
                   "The Psychology Behind Modern Training and Retraining
                   Techniques."
                   University of Chicago, B. S. in Education, 1956. Courses
                   included psychology, sociology, science, and Spanish.

Personal   Several articles published in personnel journals.
Recognition   Program director of local chapter, United Management Asso-
                   ciation.

Foreign   Fluent in Spanish.
Language

Personal
Data   Born 6/14/35

Salary   In low thirties.

References   Available on request.

CORPORATE LEGAL EXECUTIVES

LEGAL AFFAIRS VICE-PRESIDENT

Resume of   Nicholas G. Gannt
               429 Elm Street
               Northvale, NJ 07647   Telephone: (201) 585-1365

Summary of   Nineteen years of experience in general and specialized
Background   law. Started as general attorney in law firm. Later served
               as corporation counsel for large manufacturing company,
               advising on government and consumer cases. In recent
               years, heavy emphasis on patent and copyright law. Also
               experienced in the area of interferences, conflicts, and
               protection of trade secrets.

Objective   To become legal affairs vice-president in the headquar-
               ters of a corporation with international affiliates.

Employment   American Chemical Corporation
                                 Morristown, New Jersey

1974 to   Chief Counsel. Head this international firm's legal
present   department, where complexities of corporate affairs,
               employee legal problems, patents, and copyrights require
               daily attention. Advise on all corporate legal affairs,
               judging possibilities of suing and being sued.

               Correct specifications to secure proper patents after
               Food and Drug Administration has licensed production of
               specific products. Supervise proceedings before U.S.
               Patent Office and U.S. Court of Customs and Patent
               Appeals.

               Supervise copyrighting of technical specifications when
               published in booklet form and insure that these copyrights
               and patents are respected in foreign markets.

                               Bag Manufacturing Corp.
                                   Cleveland, Ohio

1968 to   Corporation Lawyer. Advised corporation concerning con-
1974   stitutional statutes, previous court decisions, ordinan-
               ces, and opinions of quasi-judicial bodies.

               Made recommendations on advisability of prosecuting or
               defending lawsuits. Acted as corporation's agent in
               various transactions of vital importance to the firm.
               Acted to keep the corporation out of expensive litigation.

Page 1 of 2

Model Resumes for Corporate and Management Executives   **81**

Freeman, Watson, and Carroll
Chicago, Illinois

1961 to 1968	General Attorney. Handled varied legal problems for firm's individual clients and for business firms and other organizations. Worked on taxes, property transactions, and accident and other claims. Advised clients on their legal rights and obligations, and when necessary, represented them in court. Negotiated settlements out of court and represented company before quasi-judicial and administrative agencies of the government.
Education	LL.B., Cornell University, Ithaca, New York, 1961. B.A., Princeton University, Princeton, New Jersey, 1959.
Memberships	New Jersey State Bar Association Ohio Bar Association Illinois Bar Association
License	Licensed to practice before the Supreme Court of the United States.
Personal	Born 1937, in Columbus, Ohio. Married.
Salary	In the range of $65,000-$70,000.
References	On request.

<u>Resume of</u>	Gretchen L. Hoover 345 Nelda Road West Houston, TX 77037 Telephone: (713) 758-4165
<u>Summary of</u> <u>Experience</u>	Nineteen years of experience in corporate and interna- tional law. In addition to researching and preparing briefs, also appear in court when cases come to trial.
<u>Occupational</u> <u>Objective</u>	To become chief counsel for a corporation with interna- tional affiliations where my expertise in international law will be of value in the company's progress.

<u>Employment</u>
<u>History</u>

<u>Merrill, Hook and Hoff</u>
Houston, Texas

1972 to
present
<u>General Attorney</u>. Specialize in corporation and interna-
tional law. Advise clients of their legal rights and
obligations and represent them in court. Negotiate set-
tlements out of court and appear before quasi-judicial
and government agencies.

<u>Law Office of Arthur I. Vince</u>
Dallas, Texas

1966 to
1972
<u>Practicing Attorney</u>. Corporate and general legal work
involving research and preparation of cases for trial.

<u>Federal Trade Commission</u>
Washington, D.C.

1961 to
1966
<u>Legal Assistant</u>. Assigned to cases involving deceptive
trade practices and to illegal discrimination cases under
the Robinson-Patman Amendment to the Clayton Act.

<u>Education</u>
LL.B., June 1961, Harvard Law School, Cambridge, Massachusetts. Member of the International Law Club. In top
one-third of graduating class. Emphasis on corporation,
tax, and international law.

B.S. in Economics, June 1959, University of Pennsylvania,
Wharton School of Finance and Commerce, Philadelphia,
Pennsylvania. Graduated sixth in class of 92. Elected to
Beta Gama Sigma, national business honor society.

Professional Affiliations	American Bar Association Texas Bar Association
Foreign Language	Reading knowledge of Spanish.
Personal	Born 1937, Dallas, Texas Single Willing to relocate
References	Available on request.

84   EFFECTIVE RESUMES FOR EXECUTIVES AND SPECIALIZED PERSONNEL

COMMUNICATIONS PERSONNEL

PUBLIC RELATIONS MANAGER

Resume of   Anna E. Feldman
10 Bayview Drive
Westport, CT 06880   Telephone: (203) 468-2935

Summary of   Nineteen years of experience in communications as a
Experience   reporter covering a state capital, as a governmental media
planning coordinator, and public relations director for a
heavy machinery manufacturing company.

Occupational   To be associated as a public relations executive with a
Objective   nonprofit or commercial organization or a firm of public
relations consultants.

Employment   National Machinery Mfg. Corp.
History   Stamford, Connecticut

This firm is a division of a large manufacturer of heavy
machinery for the aeronautical field; it employs about 400
people, and grosses approximately $200 million annually.

1972 to   Director of Public Relations. Responsible for internal
present   and external communications, as well as supervision of the
public relations staff in the development of employee,
customer, stockholder, financial, and media communications programs.

Attend board of directors meetings and give advice on the
most effective strategy to win public and governmental
support for long-range expansion plans.

                    Housing Rehabilitation Commission
                          Atlanta, Georgia

1966 to   Media Planning Coordinator. Duties included budgeting
1972   broadcast and print media schedules, conducting public
opinion polls to evaluate popular reaction to projected
programs, establishing public information policies, and
developing close association with national and regional
media.

Page 1 of 2

Model Resumes for Corporate and Management Executives **85**

                                    Indianapolis Journal
                                    Indianapolis, Indiana

1961 to   Reporter. Covered politics in the state capital. Wrote
1966   features and news stories. Attended legislative sessions.
                Became acquainted with representatives and the governor.
                Won prize for series on crime control, an exposé of delays
                in hearing cases in court. Reader response led to reforms
                in the court system and establishment of machinery for
                speedier trials.

Education   Indiana University, Bloomington, Indiana. B.A. in Liberal
                Arts, 1961. Majored in English. Courses in public rela-
                tions and publicity, industrial relations, and public
                policy. Graduated cum laude. Ranked in top ten of class of
                3,000. Elected to Phi Delta Epsilon, national honorary
                journalism fraternity.

Professional   American Management Association
Affiliations   The Public Relations Society of America
                Industrial Publicity Asociation

Personal   Born 8/20/40.
Data   Married.
                Will relocate or travel.

Salary   In the $35,000 range.

References   On request.
and Portfolio

Resume of   Thomas B. Klint
       401 Pennsylvania Avenue, N.W.
       Washington, DC 20001   Telephone: (202) 698-9126

Summary of Eighteen years experience with private publicity firm and
Experience government agency. Wrote news releases and planned cam-
       paigns for print and electronic media. Spent five years as
       adviser to Israeli government.

Occupational To become publicity director of expanding company in need
Objective   of expertise in promotion of its product or service.

Experience   International Cooperation Administration
Highlights   Communications Media Division
              Washington, D.C.

1967 to   **Publicity Adviser.** In 1970 was sent as publicity adviser
present   to government of Israel. Instituted efficient broadcast
       methods. Trained management and production personnel.
       Prepared reference material to be used in the future.

       Worked with members of the Israeli government, from deputy
       prime minister to provincial station managers. Wrote and
       produced thirty-minute documentary film about Persian
       Gulf port. Returned to home office in United States in
       1975.

           Whitney-Zimmerman Associates, Inc.
             Syracuse, New York

1962 to   **Assistant Publicity Director.** Wrote news releases and
1967   helped plan campaigns and special promotions for news-
       papers, magazines, and broadcasts over TV and radio.

       Became familiar with printing processes, typography,
       photography, paper, inks; also makeup of brochures and
       pamphlets. Guided final copy and artwork through repro-
       duction processes.

Education   B.A. degree in Public Relations, June 1962, New house
       School of Communications, Syracuse University, Syracuse,
       New York. Courses included American history, psychology,
       English, publicity and public relations, and contemporary
       civilization. Expenses covered by Merit Scholarship.
       Campus correspondent for Syracuse Telegram.

<u>Outside</u> <u>Activities</u>	Volunteer publicity chairman for local drama club. Write feature articles on free-lance basis for Sunday supplements and national magazines. Active in Landmark Preservation Society.
<u>Personal</u> <u>Data</u>	Born April 1940. Married.
<u>References</u> & Portfolio	Professional references and portfolio on request.

88   EFFECTIVE RESUMES FOR EXECUTIVES AND SPECIALIZED PERSONNEL

Resume of   Margarite V. Miller
                 4106 Pontchartrain Boulevard
                 New Orleans, LA 70118   Telephone: (504) 524-5331

Summary of   Nine years of experience here and abroad taking dictation,
Experience   handling correspondence, and assisting in office manage-
                 ment.

Occupational   To be associated with an international firm as an execu-
Objective   tive secretary or administrative assistant to management.

Work   Hastings Industries, Inc.
Record   New Orleans, Louisiana

1975 to   Executive Secretary. Executive secretary to vice-presi-
present   dent in charge of South American oil operation. Duties
                 include handling cables, correspondence, and appoint-
                 ments; making travel arrangements and preparing expense
                 reports; and answering routine mail. Position requires
                 extensive travel in South America.

                            U.S. Department of Defense
                      Office of Assistant Secretary of Defense
                              Brussels, Belgium

1973 to   Assistant Manager. Executive secretary to Deputy Con-
1975   troller for Europe. Also responsible for preliminary cost
                 studies, preparation of spread sheets, and various cost
                 computations.

                 Traveled in several NATO countries with office team;
                 responsible for supervision of personnel loaned to staff
                 and for assembling of reports on these trips. Received top
                 secret and NATO clearance.

                             Jumbo Soap Company
                              Cincinnati, Ohio

1971 to   Secretary. Secretary to assistant manager, eastern sales
1973   division. Duties included taking dictation, writing let-
                 ters and reports, and preparing of monthly statistical
                 charts.

Education   B.A. in Foreign Affairs, Miami University, Oxford, Ohio,
                 June 1971. Graduated cum laude. Member of Phi Beta Kappa.

                 Have attended night classes at University of Cincinnati.

Foreign   Read and write French and Spanish; speak both fluently.
Languages

Personal   Born 3/21/49.
Data   Marital status: single.
                 Health: excellent.

Salary   In the high teens; open to negotiation.

References   Available on request.

90   EFFECTIVE RESUMES FOR EXECUTIVES AND SPECIALIZED PERSONNEL

EXECUTIVE VICE-PRESIDENT FOR OVERSEAS OPERATIONS

Resume of   Carlton D. Dowd
1089 Appletree
Philadelphia, PA 19107   Telephone (215) 274-2916

Summary of
Experience   Over twenty years of experience in overseas marketing.
Organized International Marketing Congress. Established
sales offices abroad for international companies. Provided material for advertising and promotion of products
for South American licensees.

Occupational
Objective   To serve as executive vice-president for overseas operations of international company.

Experience   Meredith, Queen, Inc.
                   Philadelphia, Pennsylvania

1973 to
present   Licensing Coordinator. Gathered information for lectures
and programs presented for members in the United States
and abroad. Also assisted in organizing an international
Marketing Congress.

Worked on international mailings, promotional pieces, and
illustrated copy.

                  Kwick Kola, Inc.
                  New York, New York

1969 to
1973   Sales Promotion Manager, International Department.
Worked with company's foreign agents and branch managers
in Europe and Latin America, assisting in establishing and
planning the promotion for their new sales operations.
Engaged in foreign-market analysis to develop sales
organizations and to recommend promotional programs.

Issued monthly news bulletins to all foreign markets,
acting as liaison between domestic and foreign organizations.

Trained and developed sales staff in various countries in
Europe and Latin America.

Page 1 of 2

Harlequin Products, Inc.

Philadelphia, Pennsylvania

1963 to
1969

<u>Sales Manager, International Division.</u> Recruited, trained, and supervised sales representatives in New York, Washington, D.C., and the Philadelphia area.

Established company's sales organization in Germany, with headquarters in Hamburg and a branch in Frankfurt. Developed and put into operation sales organization plans. Supervised activities of field personnel; planned and conducted sales meetings; and prepared sales promotion and training manuals.

National Sales Executives, Inc.

Harrisburg, Pennsylvania

1959 to
1963

<u>Assistant Manager, International Department.</u> Helped to establish and develop international department for organization of marketing executives with expanding membership throughout the world.

Extensive liaison, trade relations, and lecturing work with members in the United States and abroad. Inaugurated, developed, and organized the International Marketing Congress.

Prepared international mailings, promotional pieces, and related literature.

Education

B.S. in Business Administration, June 1959, Temple University School of Business, Philadelphia, Pennsylvania. Majored in marketing and market research. Also studied international commercial law, economic influences on buying and selling abroad, and role of trade associations in marketing.

Languages

Fluent in English, Spanish, French; working knowledge of German, Dutch, Portuguese, and Italian.

Travel

Have traveled extensively in Europe and Latin America.

Personal
Data

Born 1937. Married, two children.

Salary

At $50,000 level, plus fringe benefits.

References

Available on request.

INTERNATIONAL SALES EXECUTIVE

<u>Resume of</u>	William M. Gonzalez 105 Cumberland Avenue Philadelphia, PA 19133 Telephone: (215) 679-9456

<u>Summary of</u>
<u>Experience</u>

Began taking orders for Christmas cards from relatives and neighbors as a child, and have been perfecting selling techniques ever since. Spent the past twenty-nine years in sales, rising from assistant manager to regional director to present post of vice-president in charge of sales. Have opened new territories for electrical appliances in Mexico, Dominican Republic, Colombia, and Venezuela. Have also worked in fields of food, paper products, and leasing of commercial equipment.

<u>Occupational</u>
<u>Objective</u>

To head overseas sales/marketing division of a multinational company.

<u>Work</u>
<u>Record</u>

<u>Electric Appliances Corp.</u>
Philadelphia, Pennsylvania

Annual sales volume for this manufacturer of electrical appliances is approximately $250 million.

1970 to
present

As <u>Vice-President in Charge of Sales</u>, my responsibilities include

— controlling and analyzing sales;
— planning and recommending operation of distribution channels;
— training of supervisory and managerial personnel in sales;
— formulating sales objectives;
— recommending pricing, conditions, and terms;
— forecasting sales, budgets, records, and statistics;
— scheduling production to meet sales requirements;
— opening new markets in Central and South America.

<u>CNY Leasing and Investment Corp.</u>
Richmond, Virginia

This corporation is one of the world's largest lessors of a wide range of commercial equipment and a major financial services corporation providing credit and credit services in more than 300 establishments with branches and subsidiaries in twenty countries.

Model Resumes for Corporate and Management Executives **93**

1964 to   As Sales Promotion Manager, my responsibilities
1970   included
               —initiating demographic surveys to determine most pro-
                  ductive markets;
               —supervising operations of six offices;
               —conducting sales training programs.

                                   Duke's Paper Co.
                                   Albany, New York

               This manufacturer of paper cups, boxes, folding cartons,
               and packaging materials employs 20,500 people. Total
               annual sales: $93 million.

1956 to   As Sales Manager, Eastern Region, my responsibilities
1964   included
               —supervising sales crew covering Eastern seaboard;
               —developing techniques for motivating staff to attain
                  increased sales.

                              Brite Life Health Products
                                 Indianapolis, Indiana

               This company distributes food supplements and household
               products through independent agents working primarily on
               part-time basis.

1951 to   As Assistant Sales Manager, my responsibilities included
1956
               — planning and conducting seminars, conventions, confer-
                  ences, and workshops in various parts of country to
                  stimulate sales;
               — establishing incentive program for sales personnel;
               — developing sales training program.

Education   B.S. in Business Administration, 1951, Paterson College,
               Paterson, New Jersey. Graduated from Washington High
               School, Jersey City, New Jersey.

Professional   Sales and Marketing Executives International
Memberships   Sales Executives Club
               National Sales Association

Languages   Mother born in Puerto Rico and family spoke Spanish at
               home. I have excellent Spanish language skills.

Personal   Born 1930, Jersey City, New Jersey. Married, one child.
Data   Excellent health.

References   On request.

94   EFFECTIVE RESUMES FOR EXECUTIVES AND SPECIALIZED PERSONNEL

Resume of   Danielle H. Arosema
                 49 Maplewood Drive
                 Forest Park, IL 60130   Telephone: (312) 756-0499

Summary of   Sixteen years experience in the export field, cor respond-
Experience   ing with buyers overseas, shipping samples and orders
                 abroad, and traveling in South America.

Occupational   Position as export sales manager with a leading industrial
Objective   manufacturer of high-quality products. Hope to assume the
                 initial responsibility for developing and maintaining an
                 effective export marketing program in foreign countries.

Work   Simon International Corp.
Record   Chicago, Illinois

1970 to   Export Sales Manager. Have increased annual sales by 40
present   percent for this manufacturer of construction equipment.
                 Continually opening new accounts through understanding of
                 international conditions and needs. Make frequent trips
                 to foreign countries to develop new contacts and maintain
                 good customer relations with established clients.

                              The Montebello Co.
                              Des Plaines, Illinois

1966 to   International Traffic Assistant. Correspondent for Latin
1970   America. Supervised shipments overseas, including all
                 consular and customs documentation.

                 Handled customers' complaints and adjustments; prepared
                 promotion material, advertising, and publications.

                 Traveled as representative to Mexico, Peru, Honduras,
                 Argentina, Colombia, Venezuela, and Puerto Rico.

                              Dimar Marketing Co.
                              Cleveland, Ohio

1964 to   Purchasing Agent. Supervised all export traffic in pur-
1966   chasing done for South American business firms. Super-
                 vised the preparation of all documentation. Saw that all
                 kinds of samples were properly and promptly remitted to
                 each firm represented. Also operated as licensed freight
                 forwarder.

Page 1 of 2

Education   Chicago University School of Commerce, Chicago, Illi-
                 nois. B.S. in Business Administration, June 1964. Majored
                 in foreign trade and international marketing.

Languages   Know English, Spanish, and Portuguese well.
                 Working knowledge of French and German.

Memberships   Export Managers Club
                 National Foreign Trade Council

Personal   Born: 11/2/42
Data   Married, two children.
                 Excellent health.
                 Willing to relocate and travel.

Salary   Open to negotiation.

References   Available upon request.

96   EFFECTIVE RESUMES FOR EXECUTIVES AND SPECIALIZED PERSONNEL

Gilbert N. Whitting
140 Stanton Avenue
Philadelphia, PA 19141

Summary of Experience

Twenty-one years of experience in army and Civilian programs translating scientific and technical books and articles to and from English, German, and Dutch. Served seven years as editor of nationally circulated Science Journal, introducing several series of articles on scientific and technical subjects based on materials originating in foreign publications and laboratories as well as innovations developing in the United States. Have perfected ability to select correct terms in making translations while retaining force of original documents.

Occupational Objective

To be connected in an executive capacity with the engineering or scientific translation division of a multinational company or nonprofit organization.

Experience Highlights

Scientific and Technical Service, Inc.
Philadelphia, Pennsylvania

1969 to present

Technical Translator. Prepare translations of English-language advertisements for placement in foreign publications; also supply English translations of technical and educational materials originating in foreign countries. In addition, I translate one technical book a year.

Science Journal
New York, New York

1962 to 1969

Science Editor. Supervised series on nuclear proliferation, pollution, and other topics of scientific and general interest for national publication established in 1889. Articles were thoroughly researched and brought wide reader response. Culled numerous foreign publications in search of scientific data to be developed. Circulation increased from 500,000 to 908,410 during the seven-year period of my editorships.

U.S. Army
West Berlin, West Germany

1959 to 1962	Liaison Officer and Interpreter between American and German authorities in West Berlin, Germany. Translated German technical documents into English and vice versa. Usually, the material pertained to technical matters in the physical and engineering sciences.

While in the army, received training in military intelligence terminology, fundamentals of intelligence, and image interpretation. Also trained in procedures for handling classified matter and military correspondence. This training supplemented my civilian background in the field of electronic engineering.

Education	Heald College of Engineering, San Francisco, California, B.S. in Electronic Engineering, 1959. Dean's list, 1958. Earned part of college expenses by holding a part-time job in electronics.

Graduated from Duluth High School, Duluth, Minnesota, 1955. Took academic course, which included mathematics and science. Also studied German and French.

Languages	Write, read, and speak fluently: English, Dutch, German (parents were foreign-born). Understand: French and Malay.

Professional Memberships	Society of Electrical and Electronic Engineers American Translators Association

Personal Data	Born 1937, Djakarta, Indonesia Naturalized American citizen Married, no children Excellent health Will relocate and travel

Salary	Open to negotiation.

References	Available on request.

Resume of	Mary V. Billings 100 Shepherd Avenue Washington, DC 20017 Telephone: (202) 675-8564
Summary of Experience	Ten years experience translating for several firms. Have worked with commercial correspondence, technical manuals, and legal contracts prepared in foreign countries. Have also served as interpreter. Have excellent working knowledge of Spanish.
Occupational Objective	To be connected with the international department of a multinational corporation as a supervisor in the preparation of translations, correspondence, technical specifications, or legal documents.

Work
Record

International Development Corp.
Washington, D.C.

**1972 to
present**

Commercial Translator. Attached to firm's international division. Its business involves more than thirty-five nations, of which twenty are Spanish-speaking, with considerable flow of Spanish correspondence. Read all foreign mail, whether in English or not. Handle all reading, translating, and answering of Spanish correspondence.

Serve as interpreter at conventions and business meetings. Listen carefully to speaker for exact meaning of his message. Translate remarks, using idiomatic language when possible in order to make presentation clear and readily understood.

American Paving Corp.
Chicago, Illinois

**1970 to
1972**

Commercial Translator. Translated legal documents and technical manuals from Spanish into English and English into Spanish. Also read and made English translations of correspondence received by the company; answered in Spanish.

Education	Syracuse University, Syracuse, New York, B.S. in Business Administration, 1970.
Personal Data	Born June 1948, Boston, Massachusetts Married, two children Willing to relocate inside or outside U.S.
Salary	Open to negotiation.
References	Available on request.

5

Model Resumes for Professionals in Science and Technology

PROFESSIONALS PROVIDE THE SCIENTIFIC AND SPECIALIZED EXPERTISE required to support managers and other supervisory personnel. They occasionally advance to managerial positions, but more often, they increase their value to employers by further developing their expertise.

Employment in scientific and engineering fields has increased more rapidly than total overall employment over the past twenty-five years. The number of scientists and engineers, for example, almost tripled, while the total number of workers in the United States grew by less than half. The growth of the scientific and technical work force is due to many factors, including overall economic growth, increased research and development expenditures by industry, and technological innovations such as the widespread use of computers.

Engineers play a prominent role in bringing scientific progress into our everyday lives. They convert raw materials and sources of power into useful products by applying basic scientific principles. Most engineers are employed by private industry, primarily by companies engaged in manufacturing machinery, electrical equipment, and aircraft and by firms providing engineering and architectural services.

Engineers design, develop, and test equipment; they also work in the production departments of manufacturing firms, or they sell technical products and provide technical assistance to customers. Some are in supervisory and management jobs in which knowledge of engineering is required.

Scientists seek knowledge of nature and the physical world through observation, study, and experimentation. The largest group of scientists are the physical scientists, who study the laws of the physical world. More than half of all physical scientists are chemists. Most work in private industry; about one-third are in chemical manufacturing. A quarter of all physical scientists are physicists. Most teach in colleges and universities. Others do research for private industry—mostly in companies manufacturing aerospace and defense products.

Life scientists study life processes and living organisms. The majority teach or do research in colleges and universities. Biologists comprise the largest group of life scientists. The medical field, which employs biologists, has grown faster than any other scientific category over the past two decades.

Mathematicians and statisticians collect, analyze, and interpret the numerical results of surveys, quality-control tests, or economic and business research programs. They assist managers and administrators in making decisions and occasionally advance to supervisory capacities.

The professional occupational field is divided into two sections. The larger group includes, among others, architects, engineers, physicians, lawyers, and teachers. It requires lengthy formal education in well-organized fields of knowledge. The other group, which includes editors, librarians, publicity directors, and technical writers, does not require specialized theoretical study but, rather, demands a broad background of knowledge and skill acquired through experience.

In either case, a college education and, preferably, an advanced degree are required for professional occupations. Licenses are needed for the practice of some professions—medicine, dentistry, and pharmacy, to name but three—and licensing authorities determine the minimum qualifications necessary for certification. In some professions, such as law, standards are also set by local bar associations that attempt to regulate the ethics of their profession's practitioners. Because of the long and intensive education and training that is required, it is difficult to enter into professional work.

Professionals should study the resumes on the following pages, using them as models for their own resumes.

Resume of   Charles H. Aldridge
                100 Stover Avenue
                Kansas City, KS 66109   Telephone (913) 698-3215

Summary of Experience

Fourteen years experience with large food production, processing, and marketing companies. Have received commendations for my machinery designs, which resulted in improved efficiency in agribusiness. Developed methods for utilizing electrical energy on farms. Experienced in specialized fertilization to achieve increased crop production.

Occupational Objective

To work with a multinational corporation that can use my services as an agricultural engineer in the United States or abroad.

Experience Highlights

Superior Cereal Co.
Kansas City, Kansas

This company produces and markets more than 800 protein foods for global distribution. Employs about 22,000 people.

1974 to present

Agricultural Engineer. My duties consist mainly of designing machinery and other equipment and developing methods to improve the efficiency and economy of the production, processing, and distribution of packaged foods for humans and animals.

International Food Co.
San Francisco, California

This food production and processing company maintains plants and distribution centers throughout the United States. Employs about 12,000 people.

1969 to 1974

Agricultural Engineer. Specialized in research and design of new equipment for processing agricultural products.

Page 1 of 2

Mid-Continent Soya Co.
Omaha, Nebraska

This company is engaged in soybean research, production, processing, and marketing. Employs more than 7,000 people.

1966 to
1969

Agricultural Scientist. Concerned primarily with soil treatment to increase soybean production. Worked on projects for increased use of electrical energy in processing plants.

Education

Bachelor of Science, 1966, College of Agriculture and Life Sciences, Cornell University, Ithaca, New York.

Military
Service

U.S. Army, 1960-1962. Honorably discharged with rank of master sergeant.

Professional
Affiliations

American Society of Agricultural Engineers
American Society of Agronomists
Agricultural Research Institute

Personal
Data

Born 1942.
Married.
Health excellent.
Will relocate.

Salary

In the range of $30,000.

References

On request.

BIOCHEMIST

Resume of   Nathan O. Miller
                   1201 Fifty-seventh Avenue South
                   Chicago, IL 60650   Telephone: (312) 336-4921

Summary of
Experience   Ten years full-time work as head of biochemical research
and development department and five years parttime
research work while studying for master's and doctoral
degrees. Have created many new products. Specialize in
preparation of new drugs.

Occupational
Objective   To head the research and development department of an
organization specializing in nutritional biochemistry
and the introduction of new biochemical products.

Experience
Highlights   **Best Products Laboratories**
                            North Chicago, Illinois

1970 to   Research and Development Vice-President. As head of
present   research and development department, I report to the
president of the corporation. Duties entail complete
analysis and testing of company's present products, as
well as development of new products.

Supervise more than eighty scientists classified under
two main sections: research section and product development section. We conduct research in various fields,
leading to the development of new products.

Supervise experimental operations carried out to create a
new product and analyze its importance and uses.

                            Balman Co.
                       Chicago, Illinois

1965 to   Research Assistant. Worked in close cooperation with
1970   physicians, bacteriologists, pharmacologists, physiolo-
gists, nutritionists, and others in development of new
drugs.

Daily routine involved trying to prepare a drug syntheti-
cally, by extraction, or by purification of natural raw
material. Gathered all equipment necessary for particular
project; this often meant construction of many types of
specialized apparatus. Raw material had to be converted to
a usable form that was suitable for case under study.

Page 1 of 2

Education   University of Chicago Graduate School, Chicago, Illi-
                     nois. Ph.D. in Biochemistry, June 1970.

                     University of Chicago Graduate Technical School, Chi-
                     cago, Illinois. M.S. in Chemistry, June 1966.

                     Massachusetts Institute of Technology, Cambridge, Mas-
                     sachusetts. B.S. in Biochemical Engineering, June 1965.

Professional   American Chemical Society
Memberships   American Institute of Biological Sciences (AIBS)
                     International College of Applied Nutrition
                     American Society of Biological Chemists

Personal   Born: 1943, Washington, D.C.
Data   Married, three children.
                     Excellent health.
                     Willing to relocate.

Salary   In the range of $40,000

References   References on request.

Model Resumes for Professionals in Science and Technology   **105**

Resume of   Harold A. Angell   Telephone: (312) 495-5869
             1254 North Dearborn Street
             Chicago, IL 60611

Summary of   Sixteen years of experience in synthetic and analytical
Experience   chemistry, with emphasis on coating technology. Assisted
             in developing many new products and processes. Acquired a
             knowledge of market research and financial analysis. Have
             been a member of scientific teams and also have acted as
             supervisor of professionals.

Occupational To be connected with a large chemical company in the
Objective   research and development laboratories; wish to be located
             within easy reach of educational institutions.

Work   Howard Chemical Company
Record   Downers Grove, Illinois

             This multinational company has annual sales of over $10
             billion, and it helped expand energy and environmental
             systems in the fossil fuels and coal conversion area.

1973 to   Chemical Engineering Development Manager. Plan and exe-
present   cute research and development programs for new products.
             Select and purchase laboratory equipment and hire techni-
             cal employees to staff technical chemical departments.
             Have been in charge of projects in the following areas:

             – management;
             – engineering;
             – process economic evaluation and
               estimating;
             – process design and engineering.

                        Starch Products International
                            New York, New York

             This firm is a major manufacturer of starch, resins, and
             adhesives; it employs about 5,000 people and grosses
             approximately $10 billion yearly.

1968 to   Product Development Engineer. Assigned as product devel-
1973   opment chemical engineer in company laboratory and plant,
             Plainfield, New Jersey. Responsible for modifications and
             research in the development of resins: vinyl acetate,
             vinyl chloride acrylate, thermosets, polyesters, and
             epoxy.

Page 1 of 2

106 EFFECTIVE RESUMES FOR EXECUTIVES AND SPECIALIZED PERSONNEL

Developed products for paper, textile, paint, protective
coatings, and related industries. Also assigned, as
technical service representative responsible for training chemists and salesmen on product line and supporting
activities of seven sales representatives. Work directly
with national firms located east of the Mississippi.

Huntsman Chemical Corp.
St. Louis, Missouri

This company is engaged in research and development,
manufacture, and sale of chemicals, plastics, petroleum
products, chemical fibers, and electronics materials and
instruments. Employs about 6,000 people. Yearly sales
average $8 billion.

1964 to
1968

Chemical Engineer. Conducted research to develop new and
improved manufacturing processes. Designed research program and oversaw workers engaged in the construction,
control, and improvement of equipment for carrying out
chemical processes for the production of better products.
Determined most effective arrangement of operations such
as mixing, crushing, heat transfer, distillation, oxida-
tion, hydrogenation, and polymerization. Supervised
workers controlling equipment such as condensers in
absorption and evaporation towers, columns, and stills.

Education

Massachusetts Institute of Technology, Cambridge, Massachusetts. M.S. in Chemical Engineering, June 1964.

Boston University School of Industrial Technology, Boston, Massachusetts. B.S. in Chemical Engineering, June
1962.

Professional
License

Licensed as Professional Engineer by State of Illinois.

Professional
Affiliations

American Society of Chemical Engineers.

Personal
Data

Born 1940. Married, three children.
Excellent health.
Willing to relocate or travel.

Salary

In the $35,000 range, plus basic fringe benefits.

References

Available on request.

CHEMIST

Wilma J. Farris
130 Tremont Avenue
Boston, MA 02135
Telephone: (617) 873-4959

Summary of Experience	Twelve years of experience as an analytical chemist, participating in development of paper, textile, paint, and protective coating products and their applications. Also worked with pharmaceuticals.
Occupational Objective	To serve as product development chemist responsible for technical research and development of new products.

Experience
Record

Universal Starch Products
Boston, Massachusetts

This firm is a major manufacturer of starch, resins, and adhesives; it employs about 2,000 people and grosses approximately $100 million annually.

1971 to
present

Product Development Chemist. Assigned as product development chemist in company laboratory and plant. Work primarily with resins. Responsible for modifications in current products and research to develop new resins.

Developed products for paper, textile, paint, protective coatings, and related industries. Also assigned as technical service representative responsible for training chemists and salesmen on product line and supporting activities of seven sales representatives. Work directly with national firms located east of the Mississippi.

Chemical Analytical Laboratories, Inc.
Cambridge, Massachusetts

1968 to
1971

Assistant Manager of Analytical Chemistry. Worked with analytical group involved with diversified projects, such as pharmaceuticals, plastics, food products, industrial cleansers, and adhesives. Became familiar with instrumental methods and conventional wet methods.

Education

Polytechnic Institute of Brooklyn, Brooklyn, New York. M.S. in Polymer Chemistry, June 1968.

Page 1 of 2

                    Lowell Technological Institute, Lowell, Massachusetts.
                    B.S. in Textile Chemistry, June 1966. Graduated cum laude.

Professional   American Association of Textile Chemists and Colorists
Memberships   American Chemical Society

Outside   Active in community politics.
Activities

Personal   Born 1944, Worcester, Massachusetts.
Data   Health excellent. Single

References   Available on request.

CONSTRUCTION ENGINEER

Jack M. Bassett
3565 Rodi Road
Pittsburgh, PA 15235
Telephone: (412) 586-2053

Summary of Experience	Supervisor and administrator, ranging from site overseer of construction project to engineer and top-level development executive. Extensive experience in design, planning, inspection, and maintenance activities plus wide experience in estimation of costs.
Occupational Objective	To be connected with an international contractor who will utilize the services of an experienced construction engineer in the completion of domestic or overseas projects.

Experience
Record

Anderson Construction Corp
Pittsburgh, Pennsylvania

1972 to
present

Construction Engineer. Worked for this international contractor for more than three years in Indonesia. Monitored contractor's performance in such important areas as on site preparation, earthwork, concrete work, underground piping, and structural steel installation.

Presently, I supervise pressure vessels, mechanical equipment, piping, and electrical instruments; however, my major duty is the supervision of the processes of piping installation.

Griffin Construction Co.
Rockford, Illinois

1963 to
1972

Corporate Buildings Engineering Manager. Responsible for management of a $10 million building program. Was responsible for the planning, coordination, and implementation of all construction activity; also worked as direct liaison executive with architect and contractors.

Gustafson & Gunther Corp.
New Brunswick, New Jersey

1957 to   Assistant Estimator. When this firm started to expand very
1963   rapidly in domestic and international operations, I was
                 hired to help in the estimation department as an assist-
                 ant. The work was concerned with construction of high-rise
                 health care facilities and other nonindustrial struc-
                 tures in this country and in the Middle East. Was in charge
                 of establishing contacts with suppliers, subcontractors,
                 and transport firms and handling all estimates.

Education   B.S. in Civil Engineering, 1957, Illinois Institute of
                 Technology, Chicago, Illinois.

                 Graduated from Forest Park High School, Forest Park, Illi-
                 nois, 1953.

Professional   Board of Directors, YMCA
Memberships   Friends of the Industrial Museum of Chicago

Personal   Born 3/17/35
Data   Married
                 Health: Excellent

References   Available on request.

Model Resumes for Professionals in Science and Technology **111**

ECONOMIST

Joan F. Mitchell
77 Park Avenue
New York, NY 10016
Telephone: (212) 678-2935

Summary of Experience	Nineteen years of experience as economist with private industry and government agency. Conduct research and make reports on domestic and international trade. Advise on operating efficiency, marketing methods, financial and fiscal problems.
Occupational Objective	To be senior economist with bank, investment house, international corporation, or government agency.

Experience
Record

Metropolitan Bank
New York, New York

1971 to
present

Financial Economist. Study and prepare reports on monetary trends, credit, and credit instruments. Help to formulate policies.

Investigate credit structures and credit collection methods. Study the interrelationships of money, credit, and purchasing power. Find ways to establish and maintain desirable balances.

Advise and consult with private industrial concerns or government agencies on operating efficiency, marketing methods, trade, and fiscal problems.

International Bank
Chicago, Illinois

1967 to
1971

International Trade Economist. Studied factors determining movement of goods among nations in order to effect favorable trade balances and establish acceptable international trade policies.

Made continuous studies of trade controls and barriers, tariffs and cartels, and import and export licensing. Determined economic reasons for restrictions.

Taught International Economics at Northwestern University School of Commerce.

112 EFFECTIVE RESUMES FOR EXECUTIVES AND SPECIALIZED PERSONNEL

U.S. Department of Commerce
Washington, D.C.

1964 to 1967	Economist. Conducted and supervised research reports on economic problems arising from production and distribution of goods and services in such fields as natural resources, utilization of assets, labor practices, credit and financing, price movements, and incidence of taxation. Compiled, organized, and interpreted economic and statistical data and devised methods for collection and processing of such data.

National Economic Marketing Service
Washington, D.C.

1961 to 1964	Market Research Analyst. Analyzed local, regional, and national areas to determine potential product or service sales according to requirements of the client or region. Studied cost of production of commodity or service in relation to supply and demand. Collected data on purchasing power, buying habits, and preferences of prospective customers.

Education 1956 to 1961	University of Chicago, Chicago, Illinois, Ph.D. in Economics, 1961. Completed required units for degree; passed comprehensive examination in banking, statistics, economic thought, international finance, public administration, accounting, industrial relations, and the social order. Met language requirements in French and German. Doctoral dissertation: "Statistical Analysis in the Field of Economics."
1955 to 1956	University of Chicago, M.B.A., 1956. General program in economics and business administration. Elective courses in advanced production problems, money and central banking, national income and employment, and public finance. Thesis: "Money and Central Banks."
1951 to 1955	Northwestern University School of Commerce, Chicago, Illinois, B.A. 1955. Majored in economics.

Model Resumes for Professionals in Science and Technology **113**

Publications   Statistical Analysis in the Field of Economics,
                University of Chicago Press, 1968.

                Advantages and Disadvantages of Investing in Latin Amer-
                ica, World Trade Academy Press, 1975.

                "International Economic Problems," Economics Association
                Review, April 1970.

                "American Abroad," International Trade, June 1974.

                "Current Problems in International Finance,"
                Harvard Business Review, Summer 1970

Personal   Born 1933. Married, four children
Data   Excellent health.
                Will relocate.

References   On request.

114 EFFECTIVE RESUMES FOR EXECUTIVES AND SPECIALIZED PERSONNEL

EDITOR

Claude J. Conway
802 Aramingo Avenue
Philadelphia, PA 19125
Telephone: (215) 677-2504

Summary of
Experience

Twenty-five years experience as reporter and editor in the
fields of business, politics, and electric and automotive
trade news. Familiar with all phases of magazine publishing from proofreading to developing article ideas and
supervising staff. Responsible for increasing circulation of Automobile News from 40,000 to 75,000 during first
five years in present post.

Occupational
Objective

To provide dynamic leadership to publication with circulation over 100,000.

Experience
Record

Automobile News
Philadelphia, Pennsylvania

1970 to
present

Editor in Chief of this monthly trade publication on
design, engineering, production, and management aspects
of automotive industries. We cover passenger cars,
trucks, buses, racing cars, test drivers, tractors,
engines, road and farm machinery, parts and components,
production, service, and maintenance equipment. Sold by
subscription and on newsstands.

Conduct monthly conference with editorial staff to discuss and plan articles for upcoming issues. Assign
projects for development by specialists in particular
phases of industry. Maintain close contact with corre-
spondents in Detroit, Los Angeles, Indianapolis, London,
Paris, Italy, Japan, Sweden, and Germany. Under my
editorial direction, pages have increased from 90 to 120
and the amount of advertising space sold has doubled.
Cooperate with circulation department in solving distribution problems.

World Wide News Weekly
Chicago, Illinois

1961 to
1970

Business News Editor in charge of content and makeup of
six-page business section of this pictorial news weekly.
Developed ideas, planned research for staff of reporters

Page 1 of 2

and photographers. Under my direction, section expanded
by 100 percent and attracted new advertising clients,
resulting in 40 percent increase in ad revenue from
business section. Introduced financial features of interest to business executives and reportage on political
issues.

Electric News Weekly
Camden, New Jersey

1955 to   As Reporter, edited and followed up news releases from
1961   manufacturers of electric equipment and appliances.
                 Covered conventions and trade shows displaying new prod-
                 ucts. Interviewed inventors and executives.

                 Advanced from reporter to Assistant Editor in 1958.
                 Assigned to do layout and supervise production. Read,
                 proof and wrote headlines.

Education   School of Journalism, University of Montana, Missoula,
                 Montana. B.A. in Journalism, June 1955. Graduated in upper
                 third of class. Courses on news editing, radio and TV,
                 industrial technology, reportage, economics, adver-
                 tising, writing, and English literature. Editor of uni-
                 versity newspaper during junior and senior years. Campus
                 correspondent for Missoula Tribune.

Personal   Born 1933. Married.
Data   Will travel; will relocate.

References   On request.

Resume of   Christie B. Huff
                    14950 Barbara Avenue
                    Cleveland, OH 44135   Telephone: (216) 495-6972

Summary of Experience

Designed and developed electronic hardware using digital techniques, integrated circuits, and microprocessors. Conducted industrial and professional experimentation in design. Supervised production of analog and digital circuits.

Occupational Objective

To be connected with a firm involved in design and development of electronic equipment where my theoretical and practical experience in the field of electronics can be utilized.

Work Record

NSE Technical Corporation
Cleveland, Ohio

1974 to present

Electronics Development Engineer. Design and develop electronic hardware using digital techniques, integrated circuits, and microprocessors. Design electronic hardware and software for medical instrumentation. Direct the efforts of staff of engineers and technicians. This position requires knowledge and experience in high-speed analog and digital circuitry, microprocessors, and solid-state sensors.

Cordovan Electrical Corp.
Chicago, Illinois

1970 to 1974

Electronics Engineer, Supervisor. Headed the electronics group of the engineering division. Supervised engineers and technicians; handled outside requests. Conducted industrial experiments in design and introduced analog and digital circuits.

Model Resumes for Professionals in Science and Technology **117**

Electromagnetic Corporation of America
Chicago, Illinois

Electrical Engineer, Head of Department. Organized
department and introduced rotating components and mag-
netic and electromagnetic devices. Developed miniature
motors and generators, and torquers, blowers, and pick-
offs, primarily for use outside company. Also developed
airborne electrical machinery, including inverters rated
from IC to 2,500 VA and alternators rated from 5,000 to
14,000 VA and machinery designed to operate at altitudes
up to 65,000 feet and at ambient temperatures from -55° to
85° Celsius.

Education   Illinois Institute of Technology, Chicago, Illinois. M.S.
in Electrical Engineering, 1967. Studied differential
equations, advanced mathematics applied to electrical
engineering, and physics. Thesis: "The Optimum Cooling
Tube for Electrical Machines: A Study in Heat Transfer."

University of Maine School of Technology, Orono, Maine.
B.S. in Electrical Engineering, 1965. Ranked in upper
quarter of graduating class of 130. Elected to Phi Beta
Kappa.

Bangor High School Bangor, Maine, graduated cum laude in a
class of 160, 1961.

Professional   American Institute of Electrical Engineers
Affiliations   Engineers' Council for Professional Development

Personal   Presently finishing work on several inventions (patents
Interests   pending).

Personal   Born 1943. Married. Excellent health.
Data

References   Available on request.

GEOLOGICAL ENGINEER

<u>Resume of</u>	James V. Thompson 520 Buckeye Avenue East Spokane, WA 99207 Telephone: (509)-9023

<u>Summary of</u>
<u>Experience</u>   Extensive experience in formulating test drilling
programs in the petroleum industry. Background in the
supervision of exploration drilling; ability and experience in preparing and interpreting the data collected in
geological surveys for further analysis by engineers and
other technical personnel. Able to determine geological
formations, related groundwater conditions, and proper
interpretation of this type of data.

<u>Occupational</u>
<u>Objective</u>   To be associated with a firm that will fully utilize my
professional background and provide potential for con-
tinued achievement.

<u>Experience</u>
<u>Record</u>   <u>United States Geological Survey</u>
                             Spokane, Washington

1970 to
present   <u>Geologist</u>. Prepare and maintain plans for engineering
geology branch of Geological Survey in Pacific Northwest;
make all public and official contacts required; provide
the basic geologic data necessary in national program of
resource development for power, navigation, irrigation,
flood control, and industrial expansion; organize geological engineering programs and projects.

Research investigations of landslides along upper
Columbia River valley in Washington. Devise new methods of
studying landslides. Have classified more than 300 landslides for statistical analysis of slide factors in
evaluating environmental geologic relationships. Study
comparisons of slide and nonslide slopes to appraise
relative stability of natural slopes. Coordinate field
and office work; write and supervise preparation of maps
and reports; select and assign personnel.

<u>United States Bureau of Reclamation</u>
Grand Coulee Dam, Washington

1965 to
1970   <u>Project Geologist</u>. Worked in concrete control section,
making mix analyses, gravel gradings, sand gradings,
moisture determinations, and silt tests; also worked in
penstock section on X-ray inspection, strain-gauge work,
records, and inspection of stress-relief welding.

Page 1 of 2

Model Resumes for Professionals in Science and Technology   **119**

Formulated test drilling program; supervised exploration drilling, followed investigations through; prepared
and interpreted data for use of designers and engineers;
determined geological formations, the related groundwater conditions, and the interpretation of these data as
they influenced engineering problems; investigated
landslide and potential landslide areas; investigated
structural relationships on basalt terrain and effects on
engineering developments; prepared reports, maps, drawings, and charts to illustrate features studied; selected
staff personnel.

Demosthenes Oil Company
Sinclair, Wyoming

1960 to
1965

Geological Engineer. Tested foundations; inspected excavations; handled field engineering in construction of a
cracking plant; supervised housing program which con-
sisted of rebuilding 275 homes and business buildings;
did petroleum engineering; inspected pressure vessels.

Did geological mapping of mines and claims; did engineering work related to mapping and mining operations at Alma
and Fairplay, Colorado.

Education

B.S. in Geological Engineering, June 1960, Colorado School
of Mines, Golden, Colorado. Followed regular curriculum,
with extra courses in petroleum and petroleum refining.

Scientific
Affiliations

Northwest Scientific Association
Geological Society of America
Listing in American Men of Science, 1970

Personal
Data

Born March 26, 1938.
Married, two children.

Salary

In the range of $30,000.

References

Available on request.

Resume of   John W. Bartlett
125 Cameron Avenue
Winston-Salem, NC 27101   Telephone: (919)227-3756

Summary of
Experience

Twenty years of diversified experience effecting cost reductions. Conducted time-and-motion studies. Served as management representative in negotiating labor contracts. Improved production through introducing improved inventory controls.

Occupational
Objective

Position as industrial engineer where my past experience and training can benefit the company and where there is an opportunity for increasing responsibilities.

Work
Record

Hill Research and Development Corp.
Winston-Salem, North Carolina

1974 to
present

Cost Engineer. My primary responsibilities include originating, coordinating, and implementing cost-reduction projects for divisions such as packing and shipping. Developed early-stage conceptual estimates for the capital cost of multimillion-dollar projects. Responsibilities include

—providing work and cost standards
—controlling production and inventory
—improving materials and handling systems
—designing facilities

Harriston, Inc
Chicago, Illinois

1968 to
1974

Industrial Engineer. This firm is a manufacturer of razors, blades, and small metal components of a precision nature. Employs approximately 800 people and grosses about $250 million a year. I started with this company as supervisor of time-and-motion studies. Responsibilities included

—having full charge of the time study division and supervision of five engineers;
—establishing a program of time studies which within eight months completely covered every job in the plant.

Page 1 of 3

One year later, I was given responsibility for the
industrial engineering division as supervising industrial engineer. Responsibilities and projects included

—having full charge of all industrial engineering
activities;
—installing a job-evaluation plan (point-factor) which
received the enthusiastic cooperation of the union;
—improving manufacturing methods, resulting in a cost
reduction of over 35 percent on one product alone;
—installing a system of tool inventory control which, by
virtue of proper systematizing of records, reduced tool
losses by 19 percent;
—preparing special cost analysis of products by operation and pointing out products which should be dropped
because of lack of volume, high production costs, or
excessive tooling charges;
—acting as management representative in several contract
negotiations.

Baker Lock Corp.
Chicago, Illinois

1965 to
1968

Industrial Engineer. This is a small lock company manufacturing special locks for industrial purposes, employing
aproximately 350 people, and grossing more than $10 million
yearly. As an industrial engineer, I

—supervised one assistant and three junior engineers;
—had complete responsibility for the establishment of
labor standards for the manufacturing and foundry
operations;
—had charge of all timekeeping and administration of the
job-evaluation plan (installed by outside consultants);
—acted as management representative in dealing with the
union;
—developed and installed a complete production-control
system.

Meridian, Inc.
Fort Wayne, Indiana

Staff Engineer. This is a well-known firm of management
consultants. As a staff engineer, I

—participated in manufacturing and sales organization
surveys, manufacturing facilities surveys, and top management organization surveys;
—participated in the survey and installation of a manufac-
turing-cost-control plan and a labor-cost determination
for installation of standard costs;
—worked on problems in the avaition, drug, dye, and
textile
fields.

Education	Northwestern University Technical School, Evanston, Illi-nois, B.S. in Industrial Engineering, 1960.
Professional Memberships	Industrial Engineering Society American Society of Mechanical Engineers American Management Association
Personal Data	Born 8/3/38. Excellent health.
References	Available on request.

Model Resumes for Professionals in Science and Technology **123**

MECHANICAL ENGINEER

George L. Boaz
149 Boone Circle North
Minneapolis, MN 55427   Telephone: (612) 428-9761

**Summary of
Experience**

Over twenty years of experience as a design and mechanical
engineer in the field of heating and air conditioning.
Have patented several products.

**Occupational
Objective**

To head mechanical engineering department of multinational corporation maintaining branches overseas.

**Experience
Record**

Metal Company of Canada, Ltd.
Montreal, Quebec, Canada

1971 to
present

Senior Mechanical Engineer. Responsible for mechanical
engineering in chemical department; supervised eight
mechanical engineers and supporting technicians. Responsible for design and development of mechanical phases of
chemical plant projects, instrumentation and electronic
devices, industrial and commercial air-conditioning,
ventilating and heating equipment, and other physical
facilities. Handles all activities from flow sheet to
sizing of pipes and piping layout to design of calculation
drawings for plant equipment and operations.

National Heater Company
St. Paul, Minnesota

1967 to
1971

Mechanical Engineer. Designed convector radiator to meet
specifications and requirements of architects for curtain
walls and other building designs. Designed electrical
heating unit and central air-conditioning units and
controls. As a result of these designs, company became
leading manufacturer of special convector radiators in
the United States and Canada. Developed several inventions; U.S. and Canadian patents granted on some; patents
pending on others.

Williams Corp.
Syracuse, New York

1959 to   Assistant Design Engineer. Helped prepare air-condition-
1967   ing and heating designs. Also assisted project engineer in
                 selling equipment to contractors. Performed functions of
                 service manager and technical adviser for large-tonnage
                 centrifugal and absorption chillers.

                 Position required imaginative designing of wide range
                 of products and equipment. Functioned as operations
                 engineer in design and construction of complete
                 petroleum-oil blending and distribution plants, includ-
                 ing plant instrumentation.

Education   B.S. in Mechanical Engineering, June 1959, Rensselaer
                 Polytechnic Institute, Troy, New York. Design and manu-
                 facturing courses: engineering drawing, manufacturing
                 processes, metallurgy, machine design, industrial engi-
                 neering, manufacturing engineering. Power generation
                 courses: chemistry, physics, dynamics of fluids, heat
                 engineering, electrical engineering, combustion, heat
                 transfer, thermodynamics.

Professional   American Society of Mechanical Engineers
Affiliations

Professional   Licensed as professional engineer in New York, Minnesota,
Licenses   and Quebec.

Patents   Device: "Hot Air Heater and Air Conditioner." Currently
                 in production.

Personal   Born 9/10/37, Glens Falls, New York. Married. Willing to
Data   relocate within United States.

References   On request.

Model Resumes for Professionals in Science and Technology   **125**

Resume of	James C. Turner
	218 River Oaks Road
	Abilene, TX 79605 Telephone: (915) 896-4321

Summary of Experience

Thorough experience in geological and geophysical surveys. Expert in analyzing earth samples and data; have knowledge of the proper derrick and drilling equipment for drilling new and old wells. Excellent background in different types of oils and their usage in the petrochemical industry.

Occupational Objective

To be associated with a forward-looking firm as petroleum engineer where well-supervision procedures, exploration and field development, and regional and detail studies are included in the responsibilities of the position.

Experience Highlights

Western Oil Company
Abilene, Texas

1970 to present

Petroleum Engineer. Devise methods to improve oil or gas production and determine need for new or modified tool designs. Study geological surveys, earth samples, and other data and advise on type of derrick and drilling equipment to be used for drilling new or reworking old wells. Oversee drilling operations and offer technical advice to achieve economical and satisfactory progress. Direct testing of bore holes to determine pressures, temperatures, direction of drilling, strata encountered, and other factors.

Prepare regular engineering reports and conduct special studies on subjects such as saltwater encroachment and operating equipment. Conduct geological and geophysical surveys.

Golden Oil Company
Fresno, California

1965 to 1970

Petroleum Engineer. This firm, one of the most efficient automated refineries in the country, produces over 400 different types of specialty oils, including plasticizers, weed killers, transformer oils, lube oils, and asphalt and asphalt rejuvenators. The plant, which employed five research chemists, was in continual change as new products were developed and old ones upgraded.

Page 1 of 2

Promoted, at substantial increase in salary, to refinery
engineer. Reported to refinery manager and vice-
president. Responsible for engineering from inception to
final installation. Supervised operating personnel during development of new products and processes.

Southern Petroleum Corporation
Maracaibo, Venezuela

1962 to 1965	Petroleum Engineer. Each year transferred to a position requiring more responsibility. In the first year, I worked in the economics and planning section, where I determined economic feasibility of new products; second year, process engineer for oil movements department, where I solved tankage and shiploading problems, designed tanks, pumps, and line-bending systems; third year, process engineer of lube solvent plant and lube packaging plant.
Education	Rensselaer Polytechnic Institute, Troy, New York. B.S. in Petroleum Geology, June 1962. Curriculum included chemistry, mathematics, physics, English, and liberal arts. Covered paleontology, petrography, petroleum geology, geophysics, groundwater geology, and reservoir geology.
Professional Affiliations	American Association of Petroleum Geologists Geological Society of America
Outside Activities	Abilene Country Club Rotary International
Personal Data	Born 1940. Married. Health excellent. Willing to relocate and travel.
Salary	At the $35,000 level, plus benefits.
References	Available on request.

TECHNICAL WRITER

Resume of   Kathleen P. Bobasch
                   441 West 105th Street
                   New York, NY 10025   Telephone: (212) 722-9546

Summary of   Wrote and supervised production of technical bulletins,
Experience   brochures, and pamphlets for leading oil, chemical, and
                   machinery companies.

Occupational   To head technical editorial department of a diversified
Objective   publishing house or the communications department of a
                   large corporation where technical materials are prepared.

Positions   Grow Chemical Corp.
Held   New York, New York

                   This company is a specialized supplier to the chemical
                   industry. The firm grosses $200 million annually and
                   employs more than 10,000 people.

1970 to   Industrial Technical Writer. Prepare instructional and
present   informational pamphlets on chemical products for
                   wholesale and retail distribution. Also edit material
                   prepared by scientists, engineers, and other technical
                   specialists.

                   Research into subject is one major duty; I also study
                   reports, read technical journals, and consult with engi-
                   neers, scientists, and other technical personnel to get a
                   clear picture of the subject being presented.

                             Hamilton Richfield Corp.
                               New York, New York

                   This is a major oil company with total assets of over $2
                   billion that markets a full line of petroleum products and
                   a variety of petrochemicals. Crude oil reserves here and
                   abroad now approach one billion barrels. Employs about
                   20,000 people.

1964 to   Technical Advertising Writer. Wrote technical advertis-
1970   ing bulletins and informational materials on products and
                   their applications for middle management and operations
                   personnel. Bulletins required acquaintance with wide
                   variety of industrial applications.

Approach varied from direct product promotion to dissemi-
nation of educational materials for new maintenance
workers and technical students.

Functions ranged from researching subjects, writing copy,
choosing and supervising photography, to specifying type.

Education
Columbia University, Graduate School. New York, New
York. M.A. in Communications, 1964. Concentrated on
writing, with special emphasis on preparing, interpreting, and writing about science and technology. Master's
thesis: "Technical Writing in American Industry."
Expenses financed with own funds.

Purdue University, Lafayette, Indiana. B.S. in
Engineering, with honors, 1962. Majored in mechanical
engineering. Senior thesis: "Functional Design for Modern Industry." Ranked in upper tenth of graduating class
of 380. Elected to Phi Beta Kappa.

**Outside
Activities**
Rotary International
New York Urban League
Planning Conference Board

**Professional
Affiliations**
Society of Technical Writers and Publishers
American Society of Mechanical Engineers
National Association of Science Writers

**Personal
Data**
Born 6/2/41. Married, no children. Willing to relocate.

**References
and Portfolio**
References and portfolio of writings available on
request.

Resume of	Arnold R. Jorgeson
	71 Park Terrace West
	New York, NY 10029

Telephone: (212) 867-5871

Summary

I am able to think in terms of spatial relationships and to visualize the effects of plans and designs. I am flexible in the approach to the solution of practical problems and appreciate the need for cooperation. I am able to exercise a high degree of independent judgment, as in suggesting or outlining studies or designing physical layout of a project.

Occupational Objective

To be associated with a public or private organization where land beautification and planning are the firm's major purposes.

Positions Held

New York State Planning Board
New York, New York

The New York State Planning Board is responsible for the general improvement and beautification of state parks and other state properties.

1968 to present

Urban Planner. Responsible for assembling information about project areas before long-range development plans can be presented for consideration and approval.

The work entails preparing studies, including maps and charts, that show current use of land for residential, business, or community purposes, arrangement of streets, highways, and water and sewer lines, and location of community facilities such as schools, libraries, and playgrounds.

These studies also provide information on various community industries, condition of buildings in each area of the city, population densities and characteristics, income levels, employment and economic trends, and other related information.

Analyzed and evaluated present conditions of area and developed plans for necessary recommendations.

Page 1 of 3

New York City Planning Commission
New York, New York

This commission is a city organization for the landscaping
of parks, gardens, scenic roads, housing projects, cam-
puses, and public clubs.

1965 to
1968

Landscape Architect. Planned entire site arrangement and
supervised grading, construction, and planning required
to complete project.

Began project by studying its nature and purpose and the
various types of structures needed. Observed and mapped
such features as slope of land and position of existing
buildings and trees. Gave consideration to views, parts
of site that would be sunny or shaded at different times of
day, structure of soil, existing utilities, and many other
factors.

Preliminary plans drawn after extensive research and
consultation with project engineer. After study and
observation, final plans were drawn.

1963 to
1965

P. C. Russell & Partners
Victoria, Hong Kong

Architectural Consultant with firm offering quantity
surveying/estimating service to architects and contractors; supervised a staff of ten. Other duties included
liaison with architects and engineers, value engineering,
postcontract work, negotiation of contract prices, investigation into investment proposals (feasibility and
development). Was offered a partnership but refused in
order to take position with New York City Planning
Commission.

Education

Rensselaer Polytechnic Institute, Troy, New York. Bachelor of Architecture in City Planning, June 1961. Studied
regular five-year course in architecture in accordance
with Architectural Accrediting Board standards. In addition to required basic courses, took survey of architectural design, site engineering, art and architecture,
city planning seminar, aesthetics, engineering geology,
industrial psychology. Took part in athletics. College
expenses financed with partial scholarship and family
allowance.

Page 2 of 3

Military   U.S. Air Force, 1961-1963. Honorably discharged; no
Service   reserve obligations.

Professional   American Institute of Architects
Affiliations   American Society of Landscape Architects
                  Urban Land Institute
                  New York State Architectural Society

Occupational   New York State License of Architecture, 1963
Licenses

Outside   Very active in church and philanthropic activities.
Activities

Personal   Born 7/14/38.
Data   Excellent health.
                  Willing to relocate.

References   References and portfolio of work available on request.
and Portfolio

6

Additional Model Resumes for Professionals

ADVERTISING ACCOUNT EXECUTIVE

Thomas A. White
325 East Sixty-fourth Street
New York, NY 10022
(212) 685-6858

Summary of
Experience

Experienced in handling liaison operations between the
agency and its clients. Studied the clients' sales and
advertising problems and developed plans to meet the
clients' needs.

Occupational
Objective

Interested in working for an agency that has national and
international departments and foreign subsidiaries. Mot-
ivated by a desire to serve multinational companies
directly.

Experience
Record

J. Walter Thompson & Co.
New York, New York

1971 to
present

Advertising Manager. Worked under the direct supervision
of an account executive. Collected information about
products and the people who use them. Used psychology and
writing techniques to prepare copy especially suited for
electronic or print media. Worked within a broad variety
of areas.

Hill Advertising Co.
New York, New York

1964 to
1971

Advertising Research Supervisor. Assembled and analyzed
information needed for effective advertising programs.
Made studies of the uses of clients' products as compared
with competing products and the best ways of reaching
potential buyers of clients' products. The main objective
in these studies was to look for the motives and habits of
potential customers.

Education

B.A., 1964, New York University, New York, New York.
Evening courses in advertising, New School for Social
Research, New York, New York

Professional
Affiliations

Advertising Federation of America
International Advertising Association
New York Chamber of Commerce and Industry.

Personal
Background

Born 1942, New Hyde Park, New York.
Will travel; will relocate.

References

References furnished on request.

19--

134 EFFECTIVE RESUMES FOR EXECUTIVES AND SPECIALIZED PERSONNEL

ARCHITECT

William B. Nelson
80 Park Avenue
New York, NY 10016
(212) 698-3628

Summary

I have worked for the past twelve years in several architectural firms, where I acquired practical experience in design, drafting, specifications, writing, and construction administration. Attended Columbia School of Architecture. Was licensed to practice in New York State and certified in several other states under the reciprocity arrangement.

Occupational Objective

It is my ambition to be connected with a large firm of architects that offers increasing possibilities for advancement and work responsibility, as well as a commensurate salary and a percentage of the profits on projects under my supervision.

Experience Record

Salernos, Sachs and Rose Corp.
New York, New York

1974 to present

Planning Architect. Make layouts for structures, coordinating the structural and ornamental elements into a unified design. Cooperate in the preparation of models of proposed buildings to enable clients to visualize completed buildings. Help write specifications and make scale drawings and full-size detailed drawings for use by building contractors and craftsmen. Often serve as overseer of operations at the building site to insure compliance with the plans and specifications. Also take an active part in planning and supervision of the remodeling and repair of buildings.

Levy, Joyce and Knappe Associates
New York, New York

1968 to 1974

Assistant Architect. The preliminary plans that were drawn up and submitted to clients for approval were under my direct supervision. Took care that alterations suggested by client were incorporated into the final designs, including floor plans and details of the exterior and interior of building. Was responsible for insuring that

Page 1 of 2

the final designs or working drawings showed exact
dimensions of every part of structure and location of
plumbing, heating, electrical, and air-conditioning
equipment, and other facilities.

Education   B.S. in Architecture, 1968. Columbia University School of
                 Architecture, New York, New York.

Professional   American Institute of Architects
Affiliations   American Society of Landscape Architects

Outside   Active in landmarks preservation groups.
Activites

Personal   Born 1945
Data   Willing to relocate

References   References on request

136 EFFECTIVE RESUMES FOR EXECUTIVES AND SPECIALIZED PERSONNEL

BANK EXECUTIVE

Peter Strauss
436 West 85th Street
New York, NY 10024
(212) 697-8324

Summary of Experience	Major bank experience with more than ten years of back- ground in business development and commercial lending gained at major banking institutions. Experience in bank planning as it relates to general economic conditions. Have worked or trained in all departments. Have super- visory experience.
Occupational Objective	To be associated with a large bank in the loan or investment division

Work
History

National City Bank, Inc.
New York, New York

1976 to
present

Bank Manager. Develop and administer policies of organization in accordance with bank rules and regulations.
Establish operating objectives and policies to attract
more depositors. Help in the coordination of plans to
insure effective flow of work between divisions.

Continental Bank & Trust Co.
New York, New York

1972 to
1976

Assistant Manager. Continually reviewed progress and made
necessary changes in bank plans, with the approval of the
president or the executive vice-president. Directed major
financial changes in such areas as policies and salary-
and-wage schedules to insure effective operation.

Chemical Manufacturers Bank, Inc.
New York, New York

1969 to
1972

Assistant Manager. Supervised collections, especially of
monies due to the bank by individuals or business enter-
prises. Bought and sold collateral, usually in the form of
commercial papers. Supervised all stock transactions to
make sure they were handled correctly and properly
cleared.

Page 1 of 2

Additional Model Resumes for Professionals **137**

<u>Education</u>   M.S. in Banking, New York University, New York, New York, 1969.
                 B.S. in Business Administration, Columbia University, New York, New York, 1967.

<u>Professional</u>   American Bankers Association
<u>Affiliations</u>   Investment Bankers Association of America

<u>Foreign</u>   Good working knowledge of German and French.
<u>Languages</u>

<u>Personal</u>   Born 1945. Excellent health. Married, two children.
<u>Data</u>

<u>References</u>   On request.

138   EFFECTIVE RESUMES FOR EXECUTIVES AND SPECIALIZED PERSONNEL

DIRECTOR OF PURCHASING

Rebecca B. Marsh
27 Court Street
Brooklyn, NY 11215
(212) 643-1843

Summary of
Experience

Am experienced in purchasing merchandise for resale. Am
able to select and order merchandise from showings made by
manufacturers' representatives, basing selections on the
nature of the clientele and the demand for the particular
merchandise. Possess a knowledge of specialized products
made by pharmaceutical or engineering companies. Know how
to stimulate sales staff and price merchandise.

Occupational
Objective

To be connected with a firm that can use and appreciate my
ability to supervise and analyze information related to
requisitions, preliminary specifications, manufacturing
limitations, vendor facilities, and availability of
materials and equipment.

Experience Record

Allied Department Stores, Inc.
New York, New York

1975 to
present

Buying Department Manager. Acquired a great deal of
information on a variety of products and merchandise.
Anticipated customer preferences by analyzing current
best-selling items in fashion and other areas. Continually analyzed past sales records to determine the price
levels appropriate for customers and the kinds of merchandise they preferred.

National Buying Service, Inc.
Chicago, Illinois

1970 to
1975

Assistant Purchasing Director. Supervised sale of compo-
nent to the manufacturers of electromechanical and electronic devices. Had complete departmental responsibility
for working with vendors, negotiating prices, and order-
ing and timing deliveries to coordinate with production
schedules.

Alexander's Department Stores, Inc.
Bronx, New York

1967 to
1970

Assistant Buyer. Chief responsibilities included verify-
ing the quality and quantity of stock received from

Page 1 of 2

Additional Model Resumes for Professionals **139**

manufacturers, authorizing payment of invoices or the
return of merchandise, approving advertising for newspapers, and supplying to the markets information such as
price, manufacturer number, season code, and style number
for inclusion on price tickets.

Education

B.S. in Business Administration, 1967, Texas Agricultural
and Mechanical College, College Station, Texas.

Personal Data

Born 1945. Married, one child. Willing to relocate.

References

References on request.

140   EFFECTIVE RESUMES FOR EXECUTIVES AND SPECIALIZED PERSONNEL

Robert H. Crane
412 East Twentieth Street
New York, NY 10009
(212) 464-4164

Summary of
Experience

I am able to cope with the special situations and
emergencies which arise daily in every hospital and to
handle unexpected demands around the clock. I am well
informed about every hospital function and service and am
experienced in the selection and supervision of the staff
members who are in charge of all departments. My primary
concerns are with the professional services needed to care
for the patients and also with matters of business and
office operation, personnel management, public relations, volunteer services, purchasing, engineering,
maintenance, and housekeeping.

Occupational
Objective

I aspire to manage a large hospital or a similar health
organization that needs the services of an able administrator who possesses good interpersonal skills, management discipline, and a sense of social responsibility and
is performance-oriented.

Experience
Record
1975 to
present

Kingsbrook Jewish Medical Center
Brooklyn, New York
Night Administrator. Took this night position because of
the opportunity it offered to become associated with a
major medical center, a hospital with a full range of
services and a qualified staff. I am part of an innovative, aggressive administrative team working from 5 P.M. to
1 A.M.

East Side Metropolitan Hospital
New York, New York
1972 to
1975

Assistant Hospital Administrator. Was closely
associated with the day-to-day operations of the medical
and nursing staffs. Allotted the necessary personnel,
supplies, and auxiliary services. Was responsible for
organizing community campaigns, representing the hospital
at meetings, and participating in planning community
health-care programs.

1970 to
1972

Emergency Department Supervisor. Supervised the emergency department and helped the physicians plan the use of
the 850 beds. Gained extensive experience in emergency
needs and noted the importance of cooperation with the
doctors in attendance.

Page 1 of 2

Education   M.S. in Hospital Administration, Northwestern Univer-
                   sity, Evanston, Illinois, 1970.
                   B.A. in Arts and Science, 1969. Brooklyn College, Brook-
                   lyn, New York.

Professional   American College of Hospital Administrators
Memberships   Hospital Financial Management Association

Personal   Born 1947. Married. Good health.
Data

References   Available on request.

HOTEL MANAGER

Sharon B. Pedersen
1100 North Dearborn Street
Chicago, IL 60610
(312) 494-3826

Summary of Experience	Possess extensive hotel experience in managing and coordinating the activities of the front office, kitchen, dining rooms, and various hotel departments such as housekeeping, accounting, personnel, purchasing, publicity, and maintenance. Have taken active part in decisions regarding room rates, credit policy, and the hotel's effect on the welfare of the community.
Occupational Objective	Am seeking a position as general manager of a large hotel in order to assume general administrative responsibility. Chiefly interested in taking charge of a hotel that offers promotion opportunities.

Work
Experience

Ambassador North Hotel
Chicago, Illinois

1973 to
present

Manager, Front Office. Coordinate front-office activities of the hotel and resolve problems arising from guests' complaints; handle reservations and room assignments and unusual requests or inquiries; assign different duties and shifts to staff and observe their activities to make sure that the hotel's policies are adhered to; establish new operating procedures.

Bretton Hall Hotel
Evanston, Illinois

1970 to
1973

Assistant Hotel Manager. During the three-to-six month periods when the general manager was away on hotel business such as publicizing and promoting the hotel, I was responsible for the smooth running of the hotel. Answered inquiries pertaining to policies and services, greeted important guests; arranged for private telephone lines and other special facilities. One of my main duties was to interview and hire applicants for supervisory posts.

Additional Model Resumes for Professionals   **143**

Education   B.A. in Hotel Administration, June 1970. Westmont Col-
                   lege, Santa Barbara, California.

Memberships   National Association of Hotel Accountants.
                   American Hotel and Motel Association

Personal   Born 7/15/48
Data   Divorced, two children.
                   Willing to relocate.

Salary   Open to negotiation.

References   Available on request.

144   EFFECTIVE RESUMES FOR EXECUTIVES AND SPECIALIZED PERSONNEL

INSURANCE UNDERWRITING MANAGER

Charlene Esposito
411 East Twenty-ninth Street
New York, NY 10016
(212) 494-9697

Summary of
Experience

Extensive background in actuarial computations and knowledge of the application of actuarial statistics and
technical computing. Experienced in working indepen-
dently, in selling various kinds of insurance, such as
life, fire, casualty, and marine. Have full knowledge of
how to sell contracts to prospective policy buyers and am
able to explain the special features of the policies
offered. Possess extensive experience in the collection
of premiums and in supervising the record keeping of all
payments received.

Occupational
Objective

Seek a position in the insurance field that requires
proven sales success working with agents and the technical
ability to handle advanced life insurance sales.

Work
Experience

American Insurance Co.
New York, New York

1970 to
present

Insurance Saleswoman. Sell insurance to new and established clients, recommending amount and type of coverage
based on analysis of prospect's circumstances. Compile
lists of prospective clients to provide leads most likely
to produce business.

Newark Underwriters Corp.
Newark, New Jersey

1956 to
1970

Assistant to Regional Vice-President. Had the responsibilities of underwriting, servicing of major accounts,
sales of all casualty lines, including workmen's compen-
sation, personal accident insurance, fire and marine
insurance and reinsurance, as well as budgeting and
profit-and-loss analysis.

Education

Hofstra University, Hempstead, New York. B.S. in Economics, 1956. Special emphasis on marketing, actuarial
computations, English composition, psychology, speech.
Took part in intramural sports. Expenses financed through
scholarships, summer jobs, and part-time employment during the college year.

Professional   American Association of Insurance Managers
Affiliations   Association of International Insurance Agents

Personal   Active in local politics and community affairs. Very
Interests   active during the last five years in the annual Red Cross
                    drive.

Personal   Born 8/1/34.
Data   Married, no children.
                    Excellent health.
                    Willing to relocate.

Salary   Salary and commission open to negotiation.

References   References on request.

146 EFFECTIVE RESUMES FOR EXECUTIVES AND SPECIALIZED PERSONNEL

REGIONAL SALES MANAGER

James B. Boeing
104 Post Street
San Francisco, CA 94106
(415) 779-6871

Objective   Position as sales executive in a regional division of a large manufacturing company.

EXPERIENCE

Sales Promotion   Devised and supervised sales promotion projects for large business firms and manufacturers, mainly in the field of electronics. Originated newspaper, radio, and television advertising and coordinated sales promotion with public relations and sales management. Analyzed market potentials and developed new techniques to increase sales effectiveness and reduce sales cost. Developed sales training manuals.

As sales executive and promotion consultant, handled a variety of accounts. Annual sales in these firms ranged from $5 million to $35 million. Was successful in raising the volume of sales in many of these firms 35 percent within the first year.

Sales Management   Hired and supervised sales staff on a local, area, and national basis. Established branch offices throughout the United States and developed uniform systems of processing orders and sales records. Promoted new products as well as the sale of old ones. Developed sales training programs and a cataloging system involving inventory control to facilitate the movement of scarce merchandise between the different branches.

Market Research   Devised and supervised market research projects to determine sales promotion potential and the need for advertising. Wrote detailed reports and recommendations describing each step in distribution, the areas for development, and plans for sales improvement.

Sales   Sold retail and wholesale to consumer, jobber, and manufacturer; products varied from hard goods and small metals to electrical appliances.

Page 1 of 2

Additional Model Resumes for Professionals   **147**

Order   Revised, processed, and expedited orders. Served as
Clerk   troubleshooter. Set up order-control systems that were
               adopted for all branches.

Employment   1973-1977 Sales Executive
History   B. B. Brown Sales Development Co.
                          San Francisco, California
               1965-1973 Senior Sales Promotion Manager
                          Industrial Research Corp.
                          Oakland, California
               1960-1965 Salesman
                          Dunnock Brothers Electronics Co.
                          San Francisco, California

Education   University of California at Berkeley, B.S. in Business
               Administration, 1960.

148   EFFECTIVE RESUMES FOR EXECUTIVES AND SPECIALIZED PERSONNEL

RETAIL STORE MANAGER

Donald L. Campbell
102 Broadway South
Aurora, IL 60505
(312) 346-7521

Summary of Experience

Possess the ability to supervise all activities of a retail store, such as controlling and setting prices of merchandise on a competitive basis. Am experienced in selecting personnel and assigning duties. I have reason to believe, from past experience, that I possess the ability to get along with people and make them feel that they are part of a team in running a retail store.

Occupational Objective

Desire association with a chain retail store that offers promotion possibilities within the organization.

Work Record

Aurora Merchandising Corp.
Aurora, Illinois

1974 to present

Manager, Retail Store. Am responsible for the managerial duties of a retail store and supervise a staff of twelve, whom I hired and trained. Also have the authority to discharge people on my staff. Plan work schedules of staff to insure efficient, productive job performance. Also am in charge of price marking on merchandise and engage in special weekly promotion activities for the sale of merchandise.

Marshall Field Corp.
Chicago, Illinois

1971 to 1974

Assistant Manager, Retail Store. Helped to formulate price policies competitive with several other retail stores in the vicinity. Coordinated sales-promotion activities, approved advertising copy and displays, supervised inventories, handled receipts, and compiled and analyzed work reports.

Education

B.S., Roosevelt College, Chicago, Illinois, 1971.

Personal Data

Born 1949. Married. Health excellent. Willing to travel and relocate.

Page 1 of 2

Occupational Memberships	American Marketing Society Sales Promotion Executives Association
Early Background	Grew up in Highland Park, Illinois. Father an engineer with Illinois Edison Company. Attended public school and Evanston High School, Evanston, Illinois. President of senior class. Played intramural football and tennis.
References	References available on request.

150 EFFECTIVE RESUMES FOR EXECUTIVES AND SPECIALIZED PERSONNEL

SENIOR TRADE BOOK EDITOR

James H. Brocken
1199 North Sheridan Road
Chicago, IL 60626
(312)212-6970

Summary of Experience	Experienced editorial consultant. Profit-oriented, competent evaluator of manuscripts. Experienced in all phases of book publishing. Strong background in nonfiction.
Occupational Objective	Seek position as senior editor with large trade book publisher.

Work Record

<u>Frazer Publishers, Inc.</u>
New York, New York

1974 to present	<u>Associate Editor</u>. Read and evaluate nonfiction manuscripts to determine their suitability for publication and act as the final editor of the manuscript if accepted for publication.

<u>Bismark Publishing Co.</u>
Philadelphia, Pennsylvania

1970 to 1974	<u>Assistant Editor</u>. Appraised the quality of manuscripts and their suitability for publication. Made necessary recommendations or critical analysis of the manuscript for submission to the senior editor who made the final decision.
Educational Record	B.A., Yale University, New Haven, Connecticut, 1968. M.A., Northwestern University, Evanston, Illinois, 1969. Graduate courses in writing and communications, University, of Chicago, Chicago, Illinois, 1969-70..
Professional Affiliations	Association of American Publishers
Personal Interests	Keen interest in community activities and local politics.
Personal Data	Born 1946. Married, no children.
References	Available on request.

19--

Additional Model Resumes for Professionals **151**

7

Model Resumes
for Technicians

MORE THAN 900,000 MEN AND WOMEN in scientific and technical occupations assist scientists and engineers. Many of these people are employed as engineering and science technicians, broadcast technicians, drafters, and surveyors.

Their work is practical and specialized, whereas engineers and scientists are more concerned with broad concepts and overall planning. Some technical assignments, however, also require an ability to analyze and solve complex problems and to prepare reports on tests and experiments.

Research and development technicians set up laboratory equipment and help design scientific instruments. In manufacturing, technicians help test and inspect products and act as a liaison between engineering and production departments. Others sell technical products, install equipment, and provide technical services to customers.

Broadcast technicians insure the technical quality of radio and television transmission and reception. They operate and maintain sound recorders, television cameras, videotape recorders, and other electronic equipment in studios and remote-control mobile units.

Drafters prepare detailed drawings that show dimensions, material requirements, and other specifications for engineers, architects, and designers.

Surveyors measure construction sites, establish official land boundaries, assist in setting land valuations, and collect information for maps and charts.

Manufacturing industries employ more than one-half of all technical personnel, primarily in the aircraft, spacecraft, missiles, and electrical equipment areas. Other manufacturing industries employing technical executives include machinery, metal products, primary metals, and chemicals and allied products. Large numbers of people also work in the construction, transportation, engineering, and architectural fields. Public utilities, including electric light, power, and communications companies, rely heavily on the skills of technicians.

Federal, state, and local government agencies have many technicians on their payrolls. Research and teaching staffs of educational institutions are another source of employment for technical assistants.

Many branches of engineering and technical fields are in the midst of a dynamic expansion that promises numerous opportunities for the future.

Mark H. Larsen
345 Peachtree Avenue
Atlanta, GA 30308
Telephone: (404) 297-3775

Summary of Experience	Fourteen years in pest control, farm machinery design, and development of soil and water conservation systems. Have sold agricultural equipment and developed techniques for improved soil production.
Occupational Objective	To work in an agricultural program of a developing country where there is need for my specialized expertise.

Experience
Highlights

Brandon Manufacturing Corp.
Atlanta, Georgia

1970 to
present

Agricultural Engineering Technician. Design farm machinery, irrigation facilities, power and electrical systems, and soil and water conservation programs.

New York State Agriculture and Markets Department
Albany, New York

1966 to
1970

Agricultural Chemist. Worked with a variety of chemicals, drugs, and related products. Studied various types of chemicals used to prevent, control, or cure animal and plant diseases and to control pests.

Education

University of Georgia, Atlanta, Georgia. B.S. in Agricultural Engineering, 1966. Courses included seminars in methods for utilizing electrical energy on farms and design of food-processing plants.

Military
Service

U.S. Army, 1960-1962. Honorably discharged with rank of master sergeant.

Professional
Affiliations

American Society of Agricultural Engineers
American Society of Agronomy
Agricultural Research Institute, Inc.

Personal
Data

Born: 8/16/1942
Health: Excellent
Marital Status: Married
Availability: Immediate

References

Available on request.

19--

AIRCRAFT MECHANIC

William F. Norton
899 Arch Way
Riverside, CA 92506
Telephone: (714) 924-6958

Summary of
Experience

Nine years of experience in U.S. Air Force and private
industry as aircraft engine mechanic and aerial engineer.
Experience in repairing and overhauling aircraft and
aircraft engines to insure airworthiness. Replace and
assemble parts, such as wings, fuselage, tail assembly,
landing gear, control cables, and propellers.

Occupational
Objective

To be connected with an airline or aircraft manufacturer
as mechanical repairman and inspector.

Experience
Record

Universal Airplane Manufacturing Co.
Riverside, California

1974 to
present

Air Mechanic Technician. Consult manufacturers' manuals
and airline maintenance manuals for specifications to
determine the feasibility of repair or replacement
of malfunctioning of airplanes. Examine engines for
cracked cylinders and oil leaks and listen to detect
sounds of malfunctioning.

U.S. Air Force
Muroc Air Force Base, California

1971 to
1974

Aircraft Mechanic. Major duties were connected with
inspection, adjustment, test repairing, and overhauling
of aircraft engines. As a flight engineer, operated the
engines, landing gear, wing flaps, and other controls and
equipment of the aircraft. Observed flight performance of
power plants and aircraft systems and checked control
devices and indicators.

Education

Took courses in motor mechanics at Topeka Mechanical
Institute, Topeka, Kansas, 1968-1971. Graduated from
Topeka High School, Topeka, Kansas, 1968. Top 15 percent
of class of 500.

Model Resumes for Technicians **155**

Military   U.S. Air Force, 1971-1974. While in the service spent the
Service   major part of the time attending different schools gaining
                background and training in the field of airplane mechanical
                functions. Honorably discharged.

Membership   Riverside Mechanical Association

Personal   Born 3/6/50.
Data   Married, one child.

References   Available from superior's office; also discharge papers
               from service.

156 EFFECTIVE RESUMES FOR EXECUTIVES AND SPECIALIZED PERSONNEL

CHEMICAL TECHNICIAN

Anne Hussey
155 Stevens Avenue
Philadelphia, PA 19111
Telephone: (215) 567-8735

Summary of Experience	Eighteen years of experience conducting tests in laboratories and working in chemical processing plants.
Occupational Objective	Employment with a chemical firm where the services of a technician can be utilized directly in plant production operations and in designing, planning, and assembling new equipment for increased production.

Work
Record

Brandywine Chemical Co.
Philadelphia, Pennsylvania

1968 to
present

Chemical Production Technician. The principal objective of my job is to supervise processing plants using chemical or related materials, operations equipment, and controls to produce commercial products. The work is centered primarily around materials and processes, and their control. It involves chemical samplings and analyses, either in the laboratory or in plant locations, and the use of other scientific methods of measurement to control the processing and regulate the quality of the final products.

Plastics Chemical Manufacturing, Inc.
York, Pennsylvania

1962 to
1968

Chemical Technician. Under the direct supervision of three chemical engineers, carried out tests, collected and recorded data, analyzed results.

Education

A.A. in Chemistry, 1962, York Junior College, York, Pennsylvania. Graduated from Clark High School, Reading, Pennsylvania, 1960.

Memberships

Industrial Chemical Association
Society of Chemical Industry Technicians

Personal
Data

Born 1942.
Willing to relocate.

Salary

Open to negotiation.

References

Available on request.

19--

Model Resumes for Technicians **157**

CONSTRUCTION TECHNICIAN

Resume of   Richard T. Harding
254 West 180th Street
New York, NY 10033
Telephone: (212) 245-6115

Summary of
Experience

Sixteen years of experience supervising construction crews. Have supervised installation of elevators and heating and cooling systems.

Occupational
Objective

To work for an architectural or construction firm that specializes in the construction of large buildings—a concern where qualifications and performance are remunerated accordingly.

Experience
Highlights

Riverdale Construction Corp.
New York, New York

1970 to
present

Field Engineering Technician. My position entails representing the construction company in different projects in New York City. My major duties are to serve as supervisor and technical executive. I check the construction work at various stages against drawings and other specifications.

Texas Builders Corp.
Dallas, Texas

1968 to
1970

Construction Foreman Technician. Was in charge of and supervised construction crews. Duties also included the supervision of earth moving, site locating, concrete pouring, and other operations related to erecting a new building.

Arbor Construction Corp.
Jersey City, New Jersey

1964 to
1968

Maintenance Foreman Technician. As a helper to the building engineer, supervised and controlled the maintenance crews. The work included overseeing installation of elevators, mechanical plumbing, heating, and air-conditioning systems.

Education

A.A., 1960, Illinois Institute of Architecture and Construction; majored in building construction technology. Graduated Stevens High School, Chicago, Illinois, 1958.

Page 1 of 2

Military Service	U.S. Army, 1960 - 1964. Based in Germany. Honorable discharge. Have letters of commendation from superior officers.
Personal Data	Born 8/13/40. Married, three children. Excellent health.
Salary	In the $20,000-$25,000 range.
References	Available on request.

DRAFTING TECHNICIAN

Jeanne H. Roncallo
1930 Grand Concourse
Bronx, NY 10457
Telephone: (212) 499-6324

Summary of
Experience

Experienced supervisor of drafting room where employees check, trace, and translate original ideas into final form. Able to prepare rough sketches, specifications, and calculations for completion of finished project.

Occupational
Objective

To secure a supervisory position where personal experience can be adapted to mechanical design.

Experience
Record

Watson & Harris, Inc.
New York, New York

1973 to
present

Senior Drafter. Supervise detailers, checkers, and tracers in translation of ideas, rough sketches, specifications, and calculations of engineers and designers into complete and accurate working plans used in connection with producing the finished product.

Make calculations concerning strength, reliability, and cost of materials; check dimensions of parts and their relationship to each other.

Use the finished drawings and specifications to describe exact materials and processes skilled craftsmen must use on a particular job.

Marion Hartz & Co.
New York, New York

1966 to
1973

Mechanical Drafter. Duties entailed such routine work of mechanical drafting as making of detail drawings of each part shown on layout; drawings gave dimensions, materials, and any information necessary for clarity and completeness.

When tracing, made necessary corrections and prepared drawings for reproduction by tracing on transparent cloth, paper, or plastic.

160 EFFECTIVE RESUMES FOR EXECUTIVES AND SPECIALIZED PERSONNEL

Martin and Martin
New York, New York

1964 to 1966	<u>Junior Drafter</u>. Assisted in making drawings for work plans; added details of mechanical drawings from sketches or notes.

Started as tracer and copyist and was gradually given more complicated and difficult drawings. Besides general mechanical drawings, also worked on projects in structural drafting.

<u>Education</u>   Alabama School of Trades, Gasden, Alabama, 1962-1964.
Studied mechanical course.
Graduated from George Washington Carver High School,
Decatur, Alabama, 1962.

<u>Personal
Data</u>   Born June 20, 1944 Birmingham, Alabama.
Married, no children.
Health excellent.

<u>Personal
Interests</u>   Reading technical periodicals, swimming, basketball as
time permits.

<u>References</u>   References on request.

ELECTRONICS TECHNICIAN

Gilbert Warren
225 Pacific Street
Brooklyn, NY 11207
Telephone: (212) 697-2234

Summary of
Experience

Fifteen years of experience in the electronics field.
Maintain and repair equipment; design and develop plans
for new products and processes.

Occupational
Objective

To be associated with a manufacturer of electronic
components where my technical knowledge can be put to use
for mutual advantage.

Employment
History

Electronic Equipment, Inc
Jamaica, New York

1969 to
present

Industrial Electronics Technician. Take an active part in
the design, development, or modification of plans for new
products and processes under the direct supervision of the
chief electronic engineer. Also help in planning production schedule.

Electric Machinery Co.
Newark, New Jersey

1967 to
1969

Electronics Technician. Prepared and interpreted engineering plans and sketches. Assumed responsibility for
environmental tests of electronic components of systems
and for the preparation of appropriate technical reports
covering the tests.

West Electronic Corp.
New York, New York

1965 to
1967

Electronic Communications Technician. Involved with
assembly, installation, operation, maintenance, and
repair of communications equipment and systems of all
types, such as industrial and entertainment sound systems, data-processing systems, telephone dial systems,
two-way radios, and high-fidelity receiving sets.

Education   Electronics Institute of Technology, Summit Park, New
                 York, graduated, 1961. Eugene Vocational School, River-
                 head, New York, specialized six-week course as electrical
                 appliance servicer, 1962.

Military   U.S. Army, 1962-1965. Honorably discharged with rank of
Service   sergeant.

Personal   Born 1942, Maspeth, New York. Married, two children.
Data

References   Furnished on request.

INDUSTRIAL DESIGNER

Daniel Hathaway
419 Falmouth Drive
Cleveland, OH 44116
Telephone: (216) 649-7238

Summary of Experience	Have designed automobile bodies and parts as well as operator interfaces for digital computer systems. Experienced in preparing first models of designs in clay so that they can be altered easily, if need be, before making the final working drawings for the development department.
Occupational Objective	To head a designing department, preferably in the automobile industry. Seek a position which offers growth potential and challenge.

Experience
Record

Johnson Industrial Designers Corporation
Cleveland, Ohio

1970 to
present

Technical Industrial Designer. Johnson Industrial Designers is a recognized pacesetter in process-control computer systems. I designed real-time CRT terminals. In my daily work, I evaluate existing technology as it applies to unique functional requirements for human interface systems. I design and implement new systems for a variety of process-control applications.

United Motors Corporation
Detroit, Michigan

1966 to
1970

Automobile Designer. Created new designs, imaginative in relation to comfort, function, and appearance, that stimulated and achieved mass acceptance by meeting consumer needs and wants in the automobile field.

Put my ideas and sketches on paper and submitted finished drawings to superiors and department heads for final approval.

Allied Motor Company
Cleveland, Ohio

1963 to
1966

Designer in the Development Room. Consulted engineers, production supervisors, and sales and market research staff regarding auto parts that needed redesigning.

Prepared several designs from which selection could be
made by company officials. Prepared first model of design
in clay. Final working model was produced by machinists,
pattern makers, or other highly skilled craftsmen in
material suitable for finished product. After model
was approved and design adopted, item was put into
production. Over twelve of my designs are currently in
use.

W. R. Rowland and Associates
Chicago, Illinois

1959 to
1963

Industrial Designer. Designed and redesigned a variety of
products such as radios, television sets, automobile
bodies, refrigerators and furniture, accenting eye appeal
to attract customers.

Researched historical background and studied products
of competitors to help develop new products.

Education

Illinois Technical Institute, Institute of Design, Chicago, Illinois. B.S. in Product Design, 1957. Curriculum
covered planning, development, and production of well-
designed objects for human use, usually for mass production. These included furniture, appliances for home and
industry, tools and implements, and automobiles and other
transportation vehicles.

Military
Service

U.S. Navy, June 1957 to July 1959. Honorably discharged
with rank of second lieutenant.

Professional
Membership

American Institute of Industrial Design

References
and Portfolio

References and design portfolio on request.

INSTRUMENTATION TECHNICIAN

William J. Perkins
450 Market Street
Newark, NJ 07105
Telephone: (201) 832-5044

Summary of Experience	My experience is in handling technical instruments, including gauges, office machines, watches, and clocks. I repair, disassemble, clean, adjust, and reassemble. Have knowledge of testing of instruments such as hydraulic pressure-control valves. I diagnose malfunctions and fully replace faulty parts.
Occupational Objective	To work for a firm where technical background in the development and function of instruments will be useful. Qualified to serve as a supervisor of such employees as instrument makers, watchmakers, typewriter servicers, and machinists.

Experience Record	American Instruments Corporation Norfolk, Virginia
1972 to present	Instrument Tester and Adapter. Continuous testing of instrument adaptability is part of the daily work. Also test hydraulic pressure-control valves. Duties include observing and diagnosing malfunctions and disassembling, repairing, or replacing faulty parts. I am seeking a new position because the New Jersey plant is being relocated out of state.
1968 to 1972	Instrumentman. Virginia. U.S. Navy. Worked from blueprints and schematic drawings to install, overhaul, and repair mechanical instruments such as meters, gauges, office machines, watches and clocks. Had to disassemble, clean, overhaul, adjust, reassemble, and lubricate watches and clocks and office machines, also dismantle, clean, test, adjust, and assemble instruments such as precision gauges and meters which record speeds, revolutions, temperatures, pressures, and vacuums.
Occupational Training	Instruction received while in U.S. Navy included such subjects as basic machines, mathematics, hand and power tools, repair and calibration of gauges and instruments, and repair of office machines.

Education   Graduated from New York Technical Institute, New York, New
                   York, 1968. Followed program offered for technicians
                   specializing in instrument maintenance and repair. Took
                   courses that gave me practical experience in the field.
                   This background contributed to my rapid advancement while
                   training during naval service.

Military   U.S. Navy, January 1968-December 1972. Served in repair
Service   shops aboard ships and at shore stations. Honorably
                   discharged.

Personal   Born 4/7/48.
Data   Married; one child.

References   References supplied upon request

TOPOGRAPHIC SURVEYOR

Orrin N. Stevens
1201 South Boulevard
Dallas, TX 75215
Telephone: (214) 327-2184

Summary of Experience	Thirteen years of experience in army and private industry as map compiler, civil engineering assistant, topographical surveyor. Pay close attention to details; possess numbers facility, the ability to visualize objects in space, and good memory. Have good hand-eye coordination and finger dexterity, plus physical stamina.
Occupational Objective	To be associated with a company or organization where the services of an experienced geodetic technician can be utilized.

Work
Record

Geological Topographic Surveyors, Inc.
Dallas, Texas

1974 to
present

Geodetic Surveyor. Determine formulas and methods of computation to be used in surveys on basis of surveyor's notes and astronomical observations. Compute topographic data, such as exact position of point and distance between points, under varied map-construction systems; coordinate surveying and computing activities.

Continental Development Co.
San Francisco, California

This is a large land development company that lays streets and installs water mains and lighting on barren land for individual private homes.

1971 to
1974

Surveyor. Calculated latitude, longitude, angles, areas, and other information for mapmaking from field notes obtained by engineering survey parties, using reference tables and calculating equipment.

Education

Graduated, 1967, Center City High School, Center City, Texas. Made excellent grades in mathematics, particularly in algebra, geometry, and trigonometry. Also took several courses in drafting and mechanical drawing.

Military   U.S. Army, 1967-1971. Worked with survey parties, assist-
Service   ing experienced surveyors. Learned army and oral code
                  signals, surveying terminology, how to read military
                  topographic maps, and how to use and maintain the various
                  kinds of instruments and equipment. Also took a course in
                  topographic computing given by the army.

Professional   Construction Surveyors Institute
Affiliations   American Society of Topographers and Surveyors

Personal   Born 1949. Married, one child.
Data   Willing to relocate.

References   Available on request.

WATER AND WASTEWATER TECHNICIAN

Roy H. Furman
299 Twenty-second Street
Philadelphia, PA 19103
Telephone: (215) 932-4528

Summary of Experience	Eight years of experience in the field of public sanitation and water conservation: two years with the State Environmental Health Laboratory, and six with Interstate Water Supply Commission. Experienced in maintaining water conservation and erosion-control systems.
Occupational Objective	To be employed as a technician by a public agency or private firm where experience, education, and initiative in the field of environmental health, especially in reference to water and disposal of wastewater, can be utilized.

Experience
Highlights

InterState Water Supply Commission
Philadelphia, Pennsylvania

1974 to
present

Water Management Technician. Among the major duties in this position are surveying, planning, and laying out construction projects and maintaining irrigation, drainage, water conservation, and erosion-control systems.

State Environmental Health Laboratory
Newark, New Jersey

1972 to
1974

Sanitation Assistant. Worked under the direct supervision of sanitation engineer in investigation of public and private establishments to determine compliance with or violation of public sanitation laws and regulations. Specialized in contamination tests of water, food, and air.

Education	A.A., 1972, New Jersey Technical Institute, Newark, New Jersey. Graduated, 1970, Washington High School, Jersey City, New Jersey.
Memberships	American Waterworks Association American Academy of Environmental Engineering American Industrial Hygiene Association
Personal Data	Born 2/25/52. Will relocate.
Salary	Open to negotiation.
References	On request.

8

COVER LETTERS

A COVER LETTER IS YOUR PERSONAL SALES TOOL. Its purpose is to sell your qualifications to a prospective employer. The best cover letters are designed to grab the reader's attention and motivate him to set up an interview with you.

The detailed information regarding your work experience and qualifications, however, should be contained in your resume. A cover letter should merely point up either your strongest qualification or the qualification that you believe best fits the job you are seeking. It should also state that you are available for an interview and that you are enclosing a copy of your resume.

Resumes are always mailed with a cover letter. Never send a resume without a letter explaining who you are and why you are qualified for a job. You can usually find the name of the person to address by checking with reference books in the library, or phoning the company personnel office.

A cover letter is written in regular business letter form. Here are the parts of a cover letter:

1. **The heading.** This gives your address and the date. It appears in the upper right-hand corner. When using a letter on which your name and address are printed, only the date should be typed in. The first line of the heading should be typed about 2½ inches below the top border of the paper. For a shorter letter, the first line should be from two to eight spaces lower, depending on the length of the letter.

2. **The introductory address.** This consists of the name and address of the person to whom the letter is written. Its first line is flush with the left-hand margin and about six lines below the last line of the heading. The introductory address, like the heading, should be single-spaced.

3. **The salutation.** This is your greeting and you can choose from any one of the following: Dear Sir, Dear Madam, Gentlemen, My dear Mr.... My dear Ms.... The salutation or greeting is flush with the

left-hand margin, two spaces below the last line of the introductory address, or two lines above the body of the letter.

4. **The body of the letter.** This is the message. The arrangement of the body should look well-balanced on the sheet of paper. Each left-hand line should be flush, except for the first line beginning each paragraph, which you can either indent a few spaces or leave flush. Either way, the paragraphs should be at least two lines apart.

5. **The closing.** This is typed two or three spaces below the last line of the body. It should align vertically with the top line of the heading. It should not extend beyond the right margin. Most closings are as follows: Sincerely, Cordially, Yours very truly, Yours truly.

6. **The signature.** Sign your name in ink under the closing. If you know the person to whom the letter is directed, you may sign only your first name, although your full name should be typed under your signature.

Cover Letter for Electrical Contractor or Electrician

> John H. Baird
> 49 Rock Road
> Gun Rock, NJ 07452
>
> May 1, 19--

Mr. Alfred Stone
Stone Brothers Contractors
98 Jackson Street
Little Falls, NJ 07459

Dear Mr. Stone:

Having accumulated five years experience as an electrician on complicated machinery for a bottling company which recently relocated in the South, I now have a license to practice in Nassau and Suffolk counties. I have four children in school and my wife and I do not wish to move out of the state.

If you need an electrical contractor for upcoming building projects in this area, I would very much appreciate hearing from you.

Enclosed is my resume, which presents full details of my experience in installing wiring for public and private housing developments.

> Sincerely,

Cover Letter for Chemical Engineer

Roland H. Bender
112 Manor Lane
Pelham Manor, NY 10506

July 10, 19--

Mr. R.H. Rome, President
Rome and Cross Chemicals, Inc.
29 Main Street
Poughkeepsie, NY 12601

Dear Mr. Rome:

I am seeking employment as a chemical engineer with a
company of your standing. Enclosed is my resume.

If you have an opening in my field, I would appreciate an
opportunity for a personal interview. I can be reached at
the above address, or by telephone at (212) 697-5899.
Thank you.

Yours very truly,

Cover Letter for Petroleum Engineer

Theodore Cherug
409 Biscayne Blvd.
Miami, FL 33120

November 1, 19--

Mr. Harry Stein, Personnel Director
Off-Shore Drilling Co.
29 Gulf Way
New Orleans, LA 70121

Dear Mr. Stein:

Following your suggestion, I am sending with this letter a
resume of my experience.

Due to changes occurring in top management policy, I am leaving my present employer at the end of this month. I am very
much interested in a position with your organization along
the lines we recently discussed. I am available for an interview at your convenience.

Cordially yours,

Cover Letter for Market Director

Ms. Jane Calloway
129 Bank Street
West Hartford, CT 06117

August 9, 19--

Ms. Mary Appleby
Barnum Products, Inc.
2 Hudson Plaza
Albany, NY 12205

Dear Ms. Appleby:

I am interested in a position as marketing director with
a progressive company such as yours. With this in view, I
am sending my resume for your consideration.

Although I am employed at present, I can arrange for an
interview at your convenience.

Very truly yours,

Cover Letter for Hospital Administrator

Dr. Lloyd Heminway
69 Seventh Ave.
New York, NY 10011

February 27, 19--

Mother Superior Therese, Director
St. Paul's Hospital
600 East 26th Street
New York, NY 10010

Dear Mother Superior:

Herein is a copy of my complete resume of experience,
academic background, and personal details.

As you will see from its contents, I have had varied
experience in the hospital field. I am seeking a more
challenging opportunity in a larger hospital and would
very much like to be considered as an applicant for
hospital administrator.

I look forward to the opportunity of an interview at your
convenience. Thank you.

Very sincerely yours,

Cover Letter for Bank Executive

Harold S. Johnson
29 High Street
Mountain View, CA 91482

January 10, 19--

Mr. Walter Marksman,
Personnel Manager
Intercity Bank and Trust Co.
San Francisco, CA 91409

Dear Mr. Marksman:

Having done business with your bank over a period of
years, and having taken note of its efficient management,
I would very much like a position with you as a bank
executive.

The type of banking experience I have had is in the direct
line of your field of operation, and I therefore feel
qualified to undertake any related duties that might be
assigned to me.

May I request an interview at your earliest convenience?
Enclosed is a full resume of my background and experience.

Thank you.

Yours sincerely,

Ernest Marston
411 Market Place
Boston, MA 09296
(617) 247-5468

October, 10, 19--

Mr. Walter McNamara, Vice President
Beacon Insurance Co.
78 Beacon Street
Boston, MA 02169

Dear Mr. McNamara:

I am what is known as an "insurance man" and have been
ever since my graduation from the University of
Pennsylvania.

The resume that accompanies this letter supports this
statement with full details as to experience, education,
and relevant personal details.

I have lived in this area for more than ten years, so I am
familiar with its economic, political, and social
aspects. I feel that this would make me especially
valuable as an insurance underwriter manager, particularly because, as the resume indicates, I know the
insurance field, and work well with people.

I can be reached any evening at the above telephone number
or through a letter at the above address. May I hope that
you will grant me an interview?

Very truly yours,

Cover Letter for Advertising Account Executive

Helen Thomas
39 Erie Drive
Chicago, IL 60603
(212) 921-4876

March 4, 19--

Mr. Joseph Clark, President
Clark Advertising Agency
21 Pacific Avenue
Los Angeles, CA 90046

Dear Mr. Clark:

Perhaps when you note the signature on this letter, you will place me as among some of the outstanding women in the field of advertising.

From the accompanying resume you will note that I have a ten-year record of profitable success as a copywriter, administrator, and, currently, as an account executive. I am anxious to change the locality of my employment; hence, I am applying to your agency because of its location and its enviable reputation in the advertising field.

In addition to the information contained in the resume, I can submit unimpeachable personal and business references. I think an interview might be of interest to your agency as well as to myself, and I look forward to hearing from you.

Most sincerely yours,

Cover Letter for Director of Purchasing

Judity H. Hillsberg
805 Sound Terrace
New Haven, CT 06513

April 23, 19--

Ms. Sandra Kelly, Vice President
Global Resorts
12 Ocean Parkway
Atlantic City, NJ 07493

Dear Ms. Kelly:

I write this letter at the suggestion of Mr. James Gleason, from whom I learned that there is an opening in your company for a director of purchasing.

The nature of your business and the nature of my experience suggest to me an excellent opportunity for mutual satisfaction between us. I have held many jobs in the field; with each one, as you will note, I have progressed to higher responsibilities and achievements.

I now wish to become associated with a company of your size and reputation that would use my experience and abilities to the fullest extent.

May I ask for an interview at your convenience? It would be very much appreciated.

Yours very truly,

Cover Letter for Hotel Manager

Ramon Paquero
18 East Broadway
Detroit, MI 48213

September 20, 19--

Mr. John Sloane, Proprietor
Mayfair House
1096 Riverview Avenue
Grosse Point, MI 49203

Dear Mr. Sloane:

As you will note from the accompanying resume, I started out as a "houseboy" in a motel a dozen years ago. Today, I can truthfully claim to be an experienced and able hotel manager.

My reason for applying to you is that, being currently employed by one of the larger hotels, I would like to make a change and work in a smaller hotel, where I feel I would be more productive and could do more for the hotel.

While the resume that accompanies this letter is a complete record of my educational and experience background, there are some personal and intangible aspects of what I have to offer that I feel confident might interest you.

I look forward to hearing from you with a suggestion for an interview at your convenience. Thank you.

Sincerely yours,

Cover Letter for Architect

Karl Parten
2095 Midway Avenue
Pittsburgh, PA 15213

February 11, 19--

Mr. John Cutler, President
Treadwell, Baker and Rees Builders
49 East 20th Street
Pittsburgh, PA 15212

Dear Mr. Cutler:

Having been employed as architect for the city since 1970,
I am now a casualty of its current fiscal difficulties and
retrenchment.

Your firm has been suggested to me as one that might have
an opening for an architect with my particular experience,
that is, in the field of medium- and low-income housing.
As you will note from the enclosed resume, my experience
as an architect includes other fields as well, but
recently I have concentrated more on developing my
specialty.

If my experience suggests that you might be interested in
what I have to offer as an architect, I should be very
grateful for an interview at your convenience. I might add
that I have an excellent record of working well and
productively with others.

Yours truly,

Alice Biddle
Hotel Bornoria
1000 East River Drive
New York, NY 10044

December 11, 19--

Ms. Louise Jenkins, Asst. Publisher
Trout Publishing Co.
600 West 43rd Street
New York, NY 10070

Dear Ms. Jenkins:

I entered the publishing field as a trainee right after
graduating from the University of Illinois with a B.S.
degree and have since been trained in various areas of
book publishing.

For the past five years, I have been senior editor of the
children's book department for California Educational
Publishers in San Francisco. In that capacity, the books
that the department handled were not "read-to-me" books,
but were "books for the child to read." They ranged in
reading difficulty from the upper-elementary grades
through high-school level, and some of the materials
that came under my supervision were of textbook quality.

I have been very happy and productive in this post, and I
am sure that my employer has been satisfied and happy with
me and my services. It is now necessary for me to relocate
to the East for family reasons; hence, this letter and its
accompanying resume addressed to you.

I am now in New York on a two-week leave and would very
much like to hear from you with a suggestion for an
interview.

Sincerely,

Cover Letter for Regional Sales Manager

Paul Milleken
29 Harbor View Lane
Minneapolis, MN 55435

January 28, 19--

Mr. Franklin Rothenberg, Personnel Manager
World Wide Sellers, Inc.
409 Main Street
Minneapolis, MN 55432

Dear Mr. Rothenberg:

I submit with this letter a resume of my extensive
experience in the business world, particularly in the
field of sales.

As of this writing, I am particularly anxious to become
one of your regional sales managers in the Midwest, where
I have lived and worked for the past five years.

If you have an opening along the lines indicated in the
enclosed resume, I would appreciate hearing from you with
a suggestion for an interview at your convenience.

May I look forward to hearing from you by letter or
telephone? Thank you.

Yours very truly,

Appendix:
State Abbreviations
Approved by U.S.
Postal Service

State	Abbreviation		
Alabama	AL	Montana	MT
Alaska	AK	Nebraska	NE
Arizona	AZ	Nevada	NV
Arkansas	AR	New Hampshire	NH
California	CA	New Jersey	NJ
Colorado	CO	New Mexico	NM
Connecticut	CT	New York	NY
Delaware	DE	North Carolina	NC
District of Columbia	DC	North Dakota	ND
Florida	FL	Ohio	OH
Georgia	GA	Oklahoma	OK
Hawaii	HI	Oregon	OR
Idaho	ID	Pennsylvania	PA
Illinois	IL	Puerto Rico	PR
Indiana	IN	Rhode Island	RI
Iowa	IA	South Carolina	SC
Kansas	KS	South Dakota	SD
Kentucky	KY	Tennessee	TN
Louisiana	LA	Texas	TX
Maine	ME	Utah	UT
Maryland	MD	Vermont	VT
Massachusetts	MA	Virginia	VA
Michigan	MI	Washington	WA
Minnesota	MN	West Virginia	WV
Mississippi	MS	Wisconsin	WI
Missouri	MO	Wyoming	WY

Index of Resumes